READY**SET**
QUILT

LEARN TO QUILT WITH **20** HOT PROJECTS

CHERYL OWEN

Creative Publishing
international

**Creative Publishing
international**

First published in the USA and Canada in 2007 by
Creative Publishing international, Inc.
18705 Lake Drive East
Chanhassen Minnesota 55317
1-800-328-3895
www.creativepub.com
All rights reserved

President/CEO: Ken Fund
VP Sales & Marketing: Peter Ackroyd
Executive Managing Editor: Barbara Harold
Creative Director: Michele Lanci-Altomare
Production Managers: Laura Hokkannen, Linda Halls

First published in UK in 2007 by
Carroll & Brown Publishers
20 Lonsdale Road
Queens Park
London NW6 6RD

Photographer: Jules Selmes

Copyright © Carroll & Brown Publishers Limited 2007

Library of Congress Cataloging-in-Publication Data

Owen, Cheryl.
Ready, set, quilt : learn patchwork, appliqué and quilting with 20 hot projects / Cheryl Owen.
p. cm.
Includes index.
ISBN-13: 978-1-58923-342-3 (soft cover)
ISBN-10: 1-58923-342-5 (soft cover)
1. Patchwork--Patterns. 2. Appliqué--Patterns. 3. Quilting--Patterns. I. Title.

TT835.O96 2007
746.46'041--dc22   2007003469

Printed in China

10 9 8 7 6 5 4 3 2 1

CONTENTS

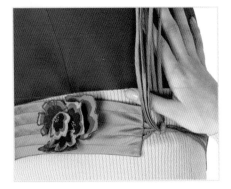

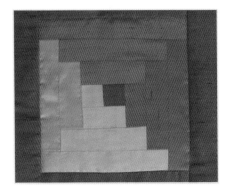
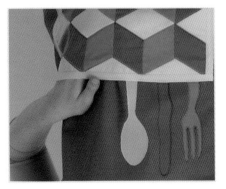
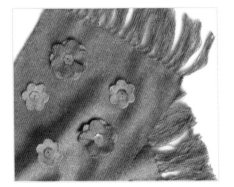

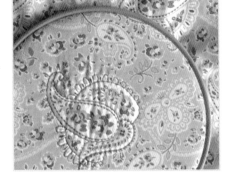

INTRODUCTION

Ready, set, quilt! In no time at all, you'll be making fabulous accessories, garments, and household items or transforming already owned plainer versions into something really special. Quilting, whether by hand or machine, is so easy to do, you'll wonder why you waited so long to get started.

Quilting has a long history as a practical craft. It can produce warm coverings for beds and bodies while patchworks and appliqués made good use of clothing remnants, turning scraps of fabric into vibrant designs and demonstrating the creative talents of generations of women.

Although they produce wonderful decorative effects, it is not difficult, even for a novice, to successfully create quilted, patchwork, and appliqué items. Inside this book, you will find everything you need to know to produce garments, personal and household accessories, and soft furnishings that incorporate traditional and contemporary motifs.

The book contains step-by-step instructions for working by hand and machine, and provides an array of quilt patterns. It also shows you how, just by stitching around printed fabric, you can produce a contour quilted design and how thread can be used even more simply to tie the fabric layers together. For more three-dimensional effects, there is information on corded and trapunto quilting.

You will be shown, too, how to piece fabric, again by hand and machine, to produce many different patchwork patterns – from square and diagonal blocks to log cabin, circular puffs or yo-yos, and the bright bands of Seminole.

Working with appliqué motifs – both hand and machine sewn – is another side to quilting. You will learn how to design, transfer, and apply them to a wide range of iitems. Moreover, you'll find out how to use lace and net to create openwork motifs.

As well as this wide range of techniques, you'll find 20 specially designed projects. There is an array of garments and personal and household accessories – ranging from a simply quilted yoga mat carrier to a wonderfully decorative special occasion keepsake picture. As well as items that are made "from scratch," you will also find out how to give new life to existing garments or items by adding decorative borders, appliquéd motifs, or lace insertions.

Quilting as a craft has stood the test of time. It's as popular today as it was for pioneer women, who used it not only to produce vital household items and garments, but also as an occasion to socialize with their neighbors. I'm certain that when you get quilting, you'll discover the many pleasures it can bring and wonder why you waited so long to begin.

Cheryl Owen

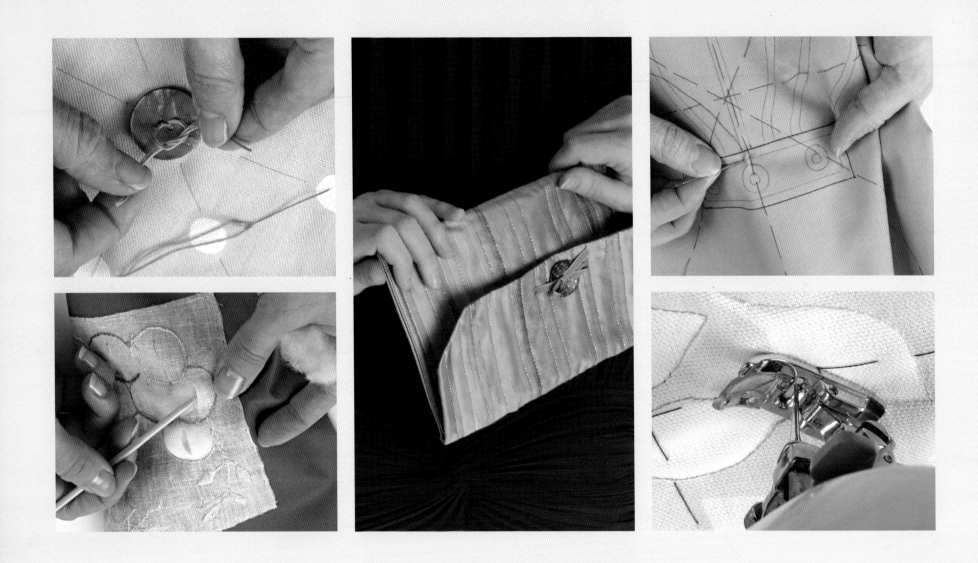

QUILTING

Warm bedcovers and stylish accessories and garments can be produced with little more than fabric and thread. In stitching fabric layers together – particularly if you use decorative patterns – you can create some wonderful surface effects. Here you will find all the techniques necessary to hand or machine quilt, from simple tied and contour quilting to corded quilting, which produces more three-dimensional designs. There are also seven beautiful projects on which to practice your quilting skills – a mix of garments, and personal and household accessories.

Quilting requires little in the way of specialist equipment, save for a hoop. When you're making patchwork, depending on the complexity of your design, you may need templates (see page 46), or a rotary cutter and board (see page 70). Quilted projects generally have three fabric layers – a top, bottom, and a middle layer of padding.

Thimble
Vital for pushing needle through three thicknesses of fabric.

Thread
Use No. 50 cotton thread for hand sewing and a No. 40 cotton thread or a polyester/cotton thread for machine sewing. Always use a 100% cotton thread for quilting.

Needles
Sharps are used for handsewing; betweens for quilting.

Pins
Fine pins with plastic or glass heads are best.

Beeswax
Strengthens thread and prevents it from kinking when hand sewing or quilting.

Embroidery scissors
Use these to clip into seam allowances or to cut thread.

Quilting hoop
A wooden hoop, with at least a 20" (50 cm) diameter, helps to keep an even tension on your work as you are quilting.

Dressmaker's shears
Use these for cutting fabric only. They should be extremely sharp.

Seam ripper
Handy for removing basting threads and unwanted stitches.

Beginners should use only 100 percent cotton fabrics, which are easy to work with, keep a crease, and wear well. Choose those with a medium weave; loosely woven fabrics have little strength and tightly woven fabrics will be difficult to quilt. Wash fabrics in hot water to test for shrinkage and colorfastness, and iron carefully before using.

Plain, striped, and patterned fabrics, including plaids, are all suitable for quilting and patchwork. Medium-scale prints, which can be compact or widely spaced are generally the best for patchwork. Small-scale prints can add a subtle texture to a design, while large-scale prints can give the impression of more than one fabric.

COLOR VALUE

In art, value is the relative lightness or darkness of a color. In patchwork, this quality can be more important than the color itself. A design can differ substantially depending upon the placement of fabrics of different values. For the best results, combine a mix of light, medium, and dark values.

In addition, color values are affected by surrounding fabrics. This can be a useful point to exploit if you are working with a limited number of colors and wish to make the best possible use of their difference in value.

GRAIN OF FABRIC

Selvages are the finished edges of fabric. The lengthwise grain, or warp, runs parallel to them and has little give. The crosswise grain, or weft, runs perpendicular to them and has a slight give. A fabric has its maximum give when it is cut on the bias, which runs at a 45° angle to the selvages. This information is essential when it comes to positioning and cutting out fabric pieces. For example, the borders of a quilt should be strong, therefore cut them with the longest edges on the lengthwise grain of the fabric. Curved patchwork should be cut with the curves on the bias of the fabric so that the pieces are easier to manipulate.

PADDING

Batting is a soft, fibrous material, used as a filling between a quilt top and back. It can be bought in a roll and comes in different widths, fibers, and weights. If you are making an item where you want to add warmth and insulation but not necessarily thickness, then you can use curtain interlining. This is a woven fabric with a soft, fleecy pile.

Selvage

Lengthwise grain

Crosswise grain

Bias

10 | Assembling a quilt

Quilts are composed of three layers – the top, the padding, and the back. Once the layers are assembled, they are basted and finally held together by hand or machine stitching or by tying.

Utilitarian quilts generally have plain fabric tops, while more decorative quilts have patchwork or appliqué on their upper surfaces. Here is an example of a log cabin patchwork basted to its backing and ready to be quilted.

PUTTING QUILT LAYERS TOGETHER

1 Measure your quilt top to determine the size of the back. Add a 2" (5 cm) margin all around (which will be trimmed off later) and, if necessary, join two or more fabric pieces to make the back.

2 Press the back carefully and lay it on a large flat surface, wrong side up. If you can, tape the edges of the back in place to prevent the fabric shifting as you work.

3 Cut a piece of batting the same size as the quilt top. Place in the center of the back. Carefully iron the top and remove any loose threads or bits of fabric. Then place it right side up on the batting.

4 Pin the layers together with long straight pins so the layers don't shift while basting.

5 Baste the layers together working from the center out to the edges, first horizontally and vertically, then diagonally in each direction. If there are any open areas of quilt remaining, secure with additional basting, working out from the center.

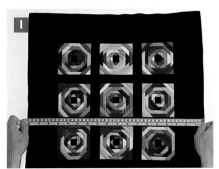

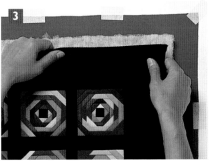

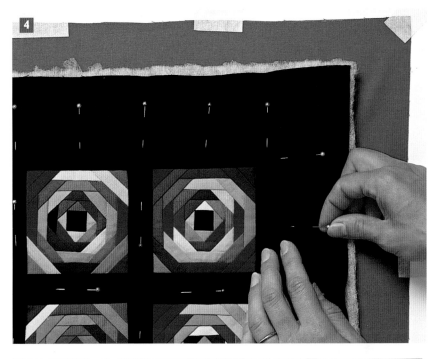

Patterns can cover the entire top or be used just for borders. The important thing is that they have evenly spaced lines — and plenty of them — to secure the padding. Border patterns work best on smaller quilted items.

The earliest quilts were often stitched in straight and diagonal lines, creating simple squares and diamond shapes. More elaborate motifs can be created using templates, stencils, or perforated patterns. The patterns shown here can be enlarged to suit your own project and transferred using the techniques on page 15. If you want to create your own designs for a simple outline shape, bear in mind that the filling lines are there to secure the batting. Always try to create an evenly spaced design.

The leaf pattern shown here is an early American wholecloth design. The leaves are made up of elaborately patterned veins surrounded by more widely spaced outlines.

PATTERNS

WHOLECLOTH MOTIFS
The Leaf (page 12) and Medallion and Clam shell designs (right) are all examples of patterns that are suitable for the entire quilt top.

BORDER PATTERNS
The Connecting hearts and Grape vine patterns (below) can be used to make a suitable border to work continuously around a quilt.

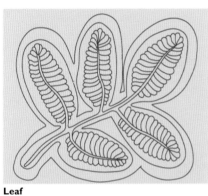

Leaf

Clam shell

Connecting hearts

Medallion

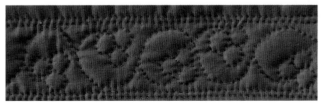

Grape vine

| # Marking patterns

There are a number of ways to transfer a quilt design to the fabric; the important thing to bear in mind is that many methods leave discernible lines that will have to be covered by your stitching.

All designs are marked on the top layer of the item to be quilted. Using chalk, silverpoint pencil, pins, or water-soluble or fading ink will produce lines that are easily removed or practically invisible, while dressmaker's carbon paper, and tracing with a regular or colored pencil will leave more permanent marks.

PRICK AND POUNCE

This is a traditional technique that is ideal to use with intricate designs. You can buy perforated patterns or draw your own design on paper. Then prick holes down all the lines of the design with a pin or unthreaded sewing machine needle. Pounce, a type of powder, is no longer available but you can use talcum powder or dust chalk. Position your design over your material and using powder or chalk on a cotton ball, rub this gently over the holes. Alternatively, you also can use a washable color marker to dot through the holes.

It's important to bear in mind that when you create your own patterns using a transfer pencil on paper, or use printed iron-on transfers, the pattern will be reversed on the fabric. You can correct this on your own designs by drawing them in mirror image.

METHODS FOR MARKING PATTERNS

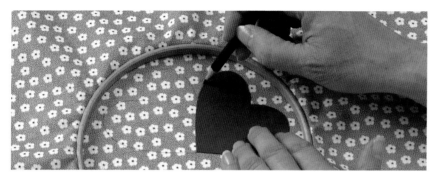

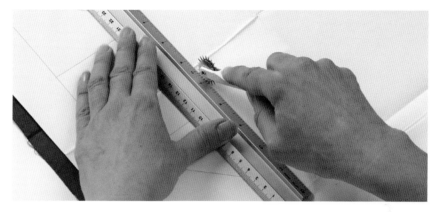

USING TEMPLATES AND STENCILS

Place your template or stencil on the fabric's right side. With a pencil, trace around the outside of the shape for a template and the inside for a stencil. If your fabric is very pale, you may be able to trace through it; in this case place your template or stencil underneath.

FOR REPEATING PATTERNS

If you are using a template to draw a repeating shape, trace from the center outward. If you like, mark the template with a notch where the shapes overlap. Make sure you first baste horizontal and vertical centering lines so you have a guide as to placing the templates evenly across your fabric.

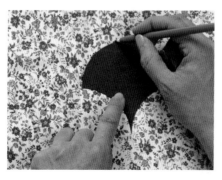

DRESSMAKER'S CARBON PAPER

Choose a color close to that of your top fabric. Lay it face down on the fabric's right side and place your pattern on top. Run a dressmaker's tracing wheel over all the lines. A dotted line will emerge. For small or intricate patterns, use a pencil or ballpoint pen instead of a wheel.

IRON-ON TRANSFERS

Transfer pencils can be used to draw a design onto paper, which can be transferred to your fabric by pressing with a warm iron. Iron-on printed transfer papers are also available; these will leave dark lines that will not wash out, so your stitching must be thick enough to cover the lines. Some quilting patterns are available with less noticeable silver-gray transfer lines.

The main purpose of quilting is to hold the top, padding, and backing layers together so they don't shift when a quilted item is being used or washed. The stitches are simple but designs can make it very ornamental.

Quilting stitches are simply running stitches that pass through all three layers, anchoring the layers together firmly. When sewing you may want to use a thimble. The simplest quilting designs are formed by parallel lines – either vertical, horizontal or diagonal, and by crossing lines, to form checks or diamond patterns. You can also buy templates for some classic motifs or transfer the ones given on page 13. Quilting helps bring your material to life by providing another design that adds dimension to your work, and serves to highlight or offset the piecing on patchworked or appliquéd items.

BASIC HAND QUILTING

1 Start by transferring your design to your fabric and pinning the top, batting, and back together.

2 Using contrasting basting thread, make rows of basting in all directions. Remove the pins. Cut an 18" (45 cm) length of quilting thread and knot the end. Insert the needle and thread through the material; pull it so that the knot becomes buried in the batting. The knot will make a popping sound as it passes through the top.

3 With the fingers of one hand below the work to help guide the needle upward, begin making a series of running stitches through the layers of fabric. The stitches should be the same length on the front and back.

4 Make three or four stitches at a time, taking the needle from the surface to the back and up to the surface again, then pull the stitches through. If you are using a hoop, you can pull firmly, which will give your stitches greater definition.

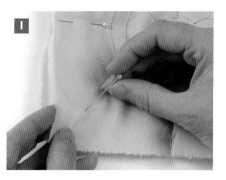

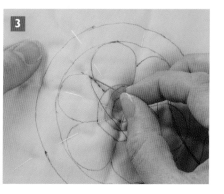

5 When you reach the end of your length of thread, make a knot close to the surface of the work. Then make a backstitch through the top and batting, pulling the knot beneath the surface and burying it in the batting.

QUILTER'S AID
If you have trouble pulling the needle through, use a balloon to grip the needle.

USING A HOOP
Quilting frames can be large and bulky, but most projects can be quilted using an embroidery hoop. Unscrew the wing nut and separate the inner and outer rings. Place the inner ring on a flat surface then position the center of your project over it. Place the outer ring over the inner, and tighten the screw after adjusting the tension. The tautness of the material in the hoop can vary from very firm to slightly pliant – experiment to find the tension you prefer.

Quicker than hand quilting, machine quilting can be an effective way to finish those pieces that are too large to stitch by hand. The secret is to maintain an even tension between the top thread and the bobbin, so test your tension on a scrap quilt "sandwich", and adjust before sewing the quilt itself. It's also very important to make the work stable by basting at regular intervals across the fabric. This is to stop the layers stretching and puckering when machining. If you will be quilting horizontally and vertically, baste diagonally and vice versa.

SETTING UP THE MACHINE

Use a size 80/12 needle, and a 50 3-ply mercerized cotton thread. Wind the bobbin with thread in a color to match the backing fabric so that any uneven stitches will not show. If the piece is well basted and not too thick, you can use a regular presser foot. If the top is being pushed ahead of the batting, use a walking foot. This contains a set of feed dogs similar to those in the throat plate.

With both sets working in unison, the fabric layers move evenly beneath the needle.

For the best result, work at a table large enough to support the entire quilt – if it hangs off the edge, it will hinder the operation. Roll large items or quilts in a scroll-like fashion and only uncover the area you wish to quilt. Secure the roll with bicycle clips.

BASIC MACHINE QUILTING

1 Cut out your top fabric, lining, and batting. Decide on how far apart you want the quilting lines. Draw lines parallel to the fold lines this distance apart, across the fabric in both directions, using a grid, an erasable marker, and ruler.

2 Pin the three layers together, starting at the center and working outward. Stabilize the work by basting a straight line down the horizontal and vertical centers of your item.

3 Stabilize the work further by basting from the center diagonally outward to the outer corners.

4 On a larger item, you need to baste at regular intervals across the work. Always baste at a different angle from the finished stitching so you don't sew over the stitches.

5 Position your needle in the marked line nearest to the center. Machine stitch along the line to the edge of the fabric.

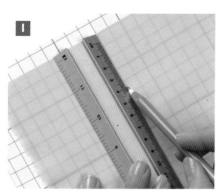

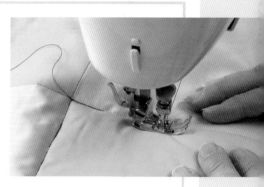

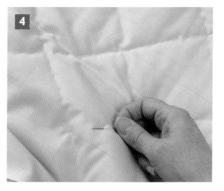

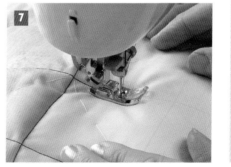

6 Cut the threads and reinsert the needle at the starting point. Stitch along the marked line in the other 3 directions.

7 Then, working from the center outward, stitch down the next parallel line. Continue, rotating the fabric, until all lines are stitched.

STITCH-IN-THE-DITCH

Beginners should try a small project first. The simplest technique is to stitch-in-the-ditch, which means to stitch along the lines of the seams on a piece of patchwork.

Adding the binding is the finishing touch that determines your quilt's overall appearance. The edges should lie smoothly without puckers or ripples. Therefore, you should bind the quilt carefully, using fabric that matches the rest of the quilt in weight and quality. The easiest method is to use commercially made bias binding but for the most interesting effect, make your own strips out of a contrasting colored or patterned fabric.

MAKING BINDING

A bias tape maker can make short work of turning under the edges of home-made bias-cut strips to make binding. You simply feed a fabric strip into the maker and it will emerge with folded sides.

ADDING THE BINDING

1 Place the middle of one side edge of the quilt on your sewing machine, right side up. Fold in one end of the binding ½" (1 cm) to the wrong side and place on the quilt top with right sides together and raw edges even. Stitch the binding to the quilt making a ¼" (5 mm) seam.

2 As you approach the first corner, shorten your stitch length and align the binding to the next edge of the quilt, leaving a fold of binding that lines up with the quilt edge. Stitch up to the edge of the fold. Stop stitching.

3 Lift the needle and the presser foot and refold the binding so that the fold is on the edge of the quilt that you have just sewn. Lower the needle exactly into the fold so that it does not catch your previous fold; lower the presser foot and continue stitching. Adjust the stitch length to normal after about ½" (1 cm). Continue machine stitching to the next corner.

4 Sew each corner in the same way. When you reach the starting point, allow the binding to overlap the beginning fold by ½" (1 cm). Trim away any excess binding.

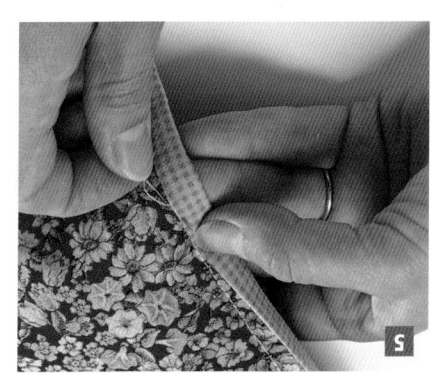

5 Wrap the folded pressed edge of the binding over to the back, overlapping the stitching line. Pin in place. Slipstitch the binding to the quilt back using matching thread.

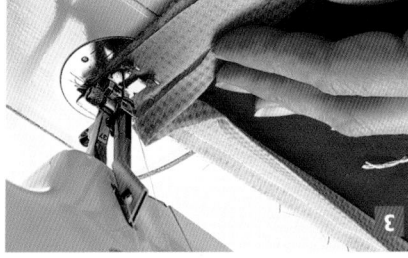

6 When you reach the end of the binding strip, fold the end of the binding ½" (1 cm) to the wrong side to make a neat join at the point the ends overlap.

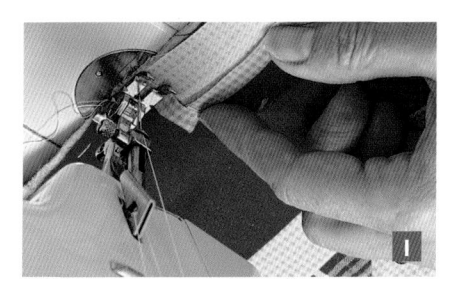

7 Use a pin to adjust the tucks at each corner into a perfect miter. Carefully stitch the mitered corners in place.

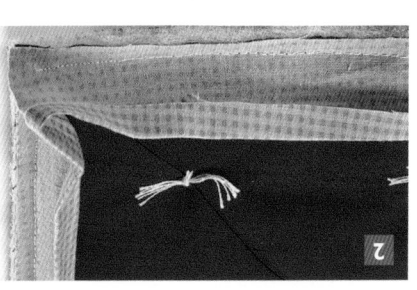

21

YOGA MAT CARRIER

This smart carrier for a yoga mat is both practical and attractive. It will protect the mat and keep it clean, and the handles make it easy to carry to classes. The quilted carrier is very simple to make; you could make another one to hold a picnic rug for summer outings.

You will need

- 32" (80 cm) cotton fabric, 44" (112 cm wide)

- 20" (50 cm) 2 oz batting

- 2⅝ yards (2.3 m) bias binding, 1" (2.5 cm) wide

- 6" (15 cm) Velcro®, 1" (2.5 cm) wide

- Erasable marker

For the holder, cut out two rectangles of fabric and one of batting, each 26" × 19" (67 × 48 cm). For the handles, cut out two 18" × 4" (45 × 10 cm) fabric strips. Round off the corners on the fabric and batting for the carrier. To do this, place a saucer at the corner and draw around the curved edge.

1 Mark your quilting pattern of diagonal lines 3" (7.5 cm) apart on one piece of fabric with an erasable marker. Sandwich the batting between your two fabric pieces so that the right sides of the fabric are outermost. Pin the layers together then baste, starting at the center and working outward.

2 If you have one, fit a walking foot to the sewing machine. Stitch along the quilting lines using quilting thread. Remove the basting and erase any marks.

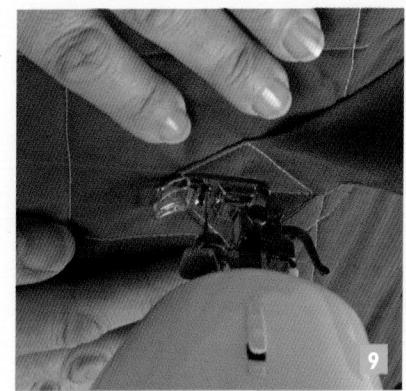

3 Trim the raw edges evenly. Stitch the binding around the edges using the slipstitch method and overlapping the ends (see page 21).

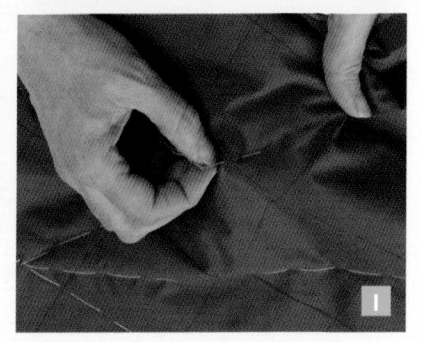

4 Pin the hook piece of Velcro® centrally, ¾" (2 cm) from one end of the holder on the wrong side. Topstitch in place close to the edge, then stitch the

Velcro® diagonally between the corners. Wrap the holder around a rolled mat and pin the corresponding piece of Velcro® to the other end of the holder on the right side. Topstitch in position as before.

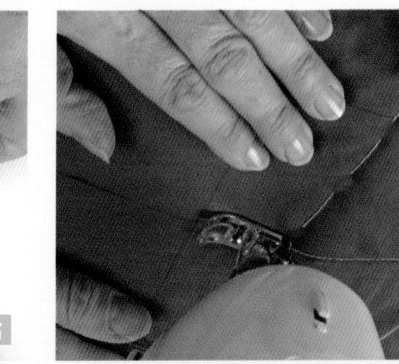

5 Press in ⅜" (8 mm) on all edges of the handles. Fold each handle in half lengthwise with right sides facing outward. Pin to secure then topstitch along the pressed edges, close to the edge.

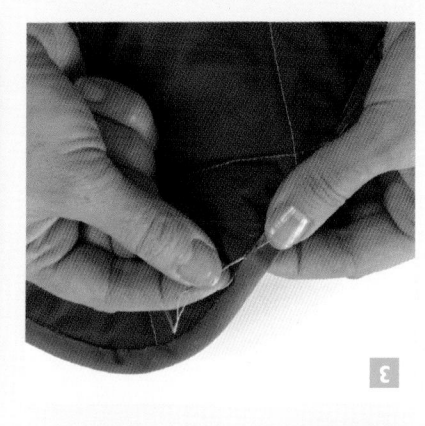

6 Pin the ends of each handle 2¾" (7 cm) from the ends of the cover and 8" (20 cm) apart on the right side. Check the position of the handles with the mat in the holder and the Velcro® fastened; adjust the handles, if necessary. Topstitch a 1⅜" (3.5 cm) square on the end of each handle then stitch a cross diagonally between the corners.

Welcome a new baby with this soft, cozy coverlet hand quilted with clouds. The clouds are dotted randomly across the fabric and it is up to you how many you have. The shapes are easy to sew if you are new to quilting. Choose a soft fabric such as brushed cotton to make the coverlet.

You will need

- 1½ yards (1.4 m) light blue brushed cotton fabric, 44" (112 cm) wide

- 1 yard (90 cm) 2 oz batting

- 4 yards (3.4 m) bias binding, 1" (2.5 cm) wide

- Erasable marker

- Even-feed foot

Using a patterned bias binding in a complementary color or colors, like the one shown here, is an easy way to add decorative interest to an otherwise plain design.

MAKING THE QUILT

Cut out two rectangles of fabric and one rectangle of batting, each 40" × 28" (100 × 70 cm). Round off the corners on each piece (see introduction, page 23). Use the template below to create the cloud shapes out of scrap paper, enlarging or reducing it as necessary. You will need about nine clouds, 6½" × 4" (16 × 10 cm) to 7" × 4¾" (18 × 12 cm).

1 Arrange the clouds on one fabric piece at least 2½" (6 cm) away from the outer edges. Pin the clouds in place and then draw around them with an erasable marker. Remove the clouds.

2 Sandwich the batting between the two fabric pieces, so the right sides of the fabric face outward. Pin the layers together then, to hold the pieces securely, make diagonal rows of basting (by hand or machine) across the coverlet, starting at the center and working outward.

3 Using matching quilting thread, make small running stitches along the outlines of the clouds. When finished, remove the basting threads and erase any marks.

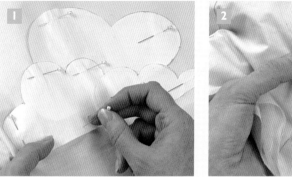

4 Trim the raw edges evenly. Using slipstitch, apply the binding all around the edge of the coverlet.

TEMPLATES

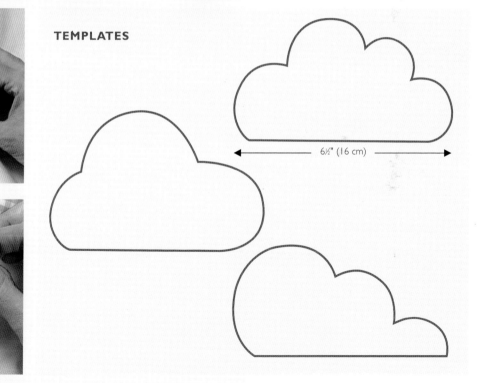

6½" (16 cm)

Quilted brocade has long been a feature of garments with an Oriental "look." Adding a border to the sleeves and hem of a plain garment is an easy way to transform the item into something more special and dressy.

You will need

- Plain jacket

- Silk brocade fabric

- Lightweight batting

- Sewing thread to match fabric

- Buttons (optional)

TIP
Choose a jacket with a boxy shape – that is one with straight sides and a straight hem, so it is easy to add a straight piece to the lower edge, without the need for any shaping.

MAKING THE JACKET

Measure the bottom hem of the jacket. Cut a strip of brocade fabric the same length plus ⅝" (1.5 cm) at both ends, for turnings, and 8¼" (20.5 cm) wide. Cut a piece of lightweight batting (in this case, curtain interlining) measuring the same length as the jacket hem and 3½" (8.5 cm) wide.

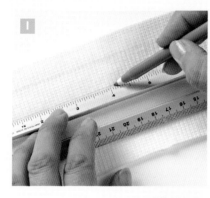

1 Mark a line ¾" (2 cm) from one long edge, along the entire length of the batting, on both sides. Then mark three more lines between these, ¾" (2 cm) apart.

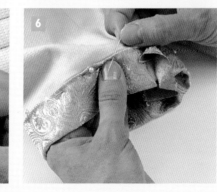

2 Pin and baste the batting to the wrong side of the fabric strip, ⅝" (1.5 cm) in from one of the long edges.

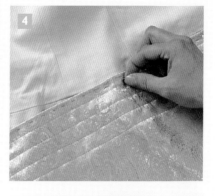

3 Machine stitch along these lines, to create lines of quilting.

4 Pin the quilted strip to the jacket. (Here there is a ribbed border that is to be completely covered by the brocade trim.)

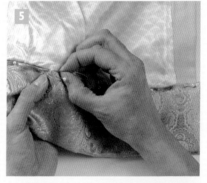

5 Turn under ⅝" (1.5 cm) on the top edge and slipstitch in place. Do the same on the inside, trimming any excess batting close to the seam line. Fold under ⅝" (1.5 cm) at both ends and slipstitch folded edges together.

6 For the cuffs, cut strips to correspond with the circumference and width of the sleeve ends, plus ⅝" (1.5 cm) all around for turnings. Attach to the sleeves by slipstitching, in a similar way to the quilted border, but without interlining or quilting.

7 If you wish, replace the jacket buttons with ones that coordinate with the fabric border you have added.

Contour quilting

Contour quilting is really very simple. Instead of quilting a design on to your fabric, you use a printed fabric for the top of your item and stitch along some of its lines. Contour quilting can be used to great effect on garments, accessories, and wall hangings.

Contour quilting works well not only on pictorial printed fabrics, such as florals, but also on stripes and abstract designs – as long as the designs are relatively big and bold. It's also effective with pre-printed patchwork fabric. It is not necessary to quilt every line on a pattern; not only is this tedious but the effect of the quilting may be lost. Choose a few bold lines to work along and, if necessary, to hold the fabrics together; use straight quilting lines on the remainder of the fabric. Experiment with the same or contrasting thread to see which gives the best result.

METALLIC THREADS
Extra sparkle can be added to printed fabrics if metallic thread is used for the quilting stitches. Use small lengths of thread (metallic threads fray easily) and running stitches made by hand along some of the dominant lines.

CONTOUR QUILTING TECHNIQUES

BASIC CONTOUR QUILTING

1 Place your backing fabric face down and top with padding. Cover with your printed fabric. Baste all three layers together with several lines of basting stitches in all directions.

2 Using a machine set to a medium-length straight stitch, start sewing the shapes nearest the center of your piece and work outward.

3 Continue sewing along the major lines, carefully changing direction and working around any irregular shapes to prevent the fabric bunching.

4 Finish off the threads neatly and securely at the end of every stitched line. Remove the basting threads.

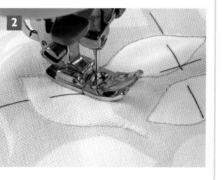

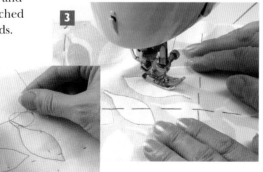

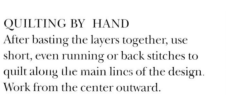

STRIPES

Decide which stripes you want to contour quilt and then use "invisible" thread to work rows of zig-zag stitches along and beween some of the others. Then straight stitch down your chosen stripes.

PATCHWORK

Pick out some of the shapes you want to make "stand out" and straight stitch around these. Don't stitch every pattern as the three-dimensional effect will be lost.

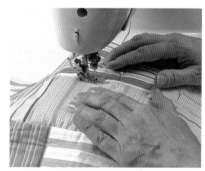

QUILTING BY HAND

After basting the layers together, use short, even running or back stitches to quilt along the main lines of the design. Work from the center outward.

A simple but stylish envelope-style bag can be created from striped silk ornamented by stitching with metallic thread along stripes of different widths. A decorative button and silk ribbon trim provides the finishing touch.

You will need

- ½ yard (45 cm) striped silk fabric

- ½ yard (45 cm) batting

- ½ yard (45 cm) silk lining

- Metallic or strongly contrasting thread

- Notions: snap, button, and ribbon

MAKING THE BAG

1 Cut a rectangle, approximately 17" × 11½" (43 × 29 cm) from your fabric, batting, and lining. Trim diagonally both corners on one short end.

2 Sandwich the fabric between the batting and the lining and stitch all three fabrics together, making a ⅝" (1.5 cm) seam allowance. Leave a large gap along one short edge. Trim seam edges.

3 Turn the bag inside out so the striped fabric is at the front. Slipstitch the gap closed then press the seams flat.

4 Make several lines of horizontal basting stitches using a contrasting colored thread to hold the fabric layers together.

5 Mark the stripes you will want to emphasize. Stripes of different widths will produce a more interesting effect than choosing ones of the same size. Using at least two strands of a metallic or boldly contrasting thread, and working from the center out to the sides, stitch down the marked lines using medium-sized stitches.

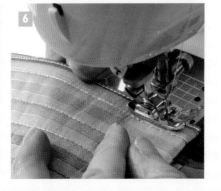

6 Fold up the short, straight edge approximately 6" (15 cm) and stitch both sides close to the edges to create the bag. Sew the ball part of the snap to the top of the bag – in the center of the back. Sew the socket of the snap in the middle of the bottom of the bag – about 3" (7.5 cm) up from the bottom.

FINISHING TOUCH
A pretty button topped with a decorative ribbon bow can be stitched to the top of the bag.

Trapunto quilting

Another form of raised quilting, trapunto involves inserting batting or a padding of soft cotton behind a motif in order to make it stand out from the background fabric. A crochet hook or a blunt-ended needle can be used to insert the stuffing. By varying the amount of stuffing used in each area, you can produce some highly three-dimensional effects.

Here, a simple heart shape turns a sachet bag into something special. You can create more intricate designs by ganging up simple shapes. However, the technique can be used successfully for more elaborate motifs.

1 Mark the design on to the front of the backing fabric, either drawing it freehand or using one of the transferring methods on page 15.

2 Baste the top fabric, right side facing outward, to a lining fabric. Stitch along the outlines of your design. If hand stitching, use a firm backstitch in a strong thread to give definition to the "pockets," you will be filling. Work from the center outward.

3 Make a small slit in the fabric at the back of each motif, being careful not to cut the top fabric. If you use a loosely woven backing fabric, you can pull apart the threads with a crochet hook rather than cut them.

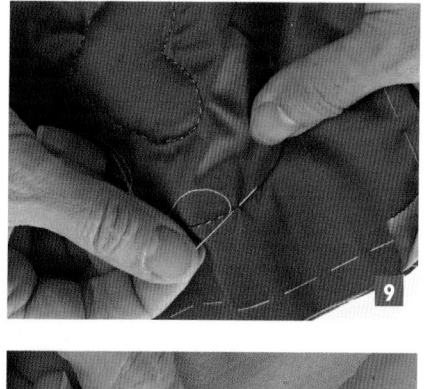

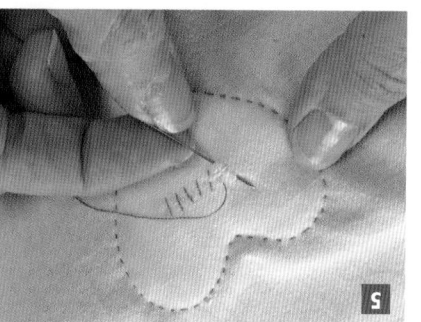

4 Insert the padding with a crochet hook or a blunt needle, taking care to position it evenly and not to overstuff the design; check the front for the effect.

5 Make overcast or slipstitches to close the slit.

6 Add backing fabric; this is necessary to protect the stuffing from falling out due to wear and tear. For a small item with a single, central motif, baste the backing, right side facing outward to the lined piece. Then echo the pattern of your motif with backstitching a short distance away from the padded design. Pink the fabric close to the outside stitching to prevent it raveling and to create a decorative edge.

TRAPUNTO BOX

Plain boxes known as "blanks" are available from craft shops. They are ideal for covering with lightweight embellished fabrics that show off your needlework skills. Here, the printed floral fabric on the base inspired the berry motifs worked with the trapunto technique on the top. The design is stitched in the floral print's colors and highlighted with a few simple embroidery stitches.

You will need

- Rectangular box blank, $7\frac{3}{4}$" $\times$ $5\frac{5}{8}$" $\times$ $3\frac{1}{2}$" (20 $\times$ 14.5 $\times$ 9 cm)

- Lightweight plain and floral-print fabrics, each $\frac{1}{4}$ yard (20 cm) of any width

- Remnant plain white muslin

- Embroidery hoop

- Erasable marker

- Acrylic paint in coordinating color and flat paintbrush

- Stranded cotton embroidery floss to match the printed fabric

- Remnant polyester batting

- Crochet hook

- Double sided tape, $\frac{1}{2}$" (1 cm) wide

- 1 yard (90 cm) ribbon, $\frac{1}{2}$" (1 cm) wide

The lengths of materials given are for a box measuring 8" $\times$ $5\frac{5}{8}$" $\times$ $3\frac{1}{2}$" (20 $\times$ 14.5 $\times$ 9 cm) but these can be easily recalculated to cover any size or shape.

MAKING THE BOX

From the plain fabric, cut a rectangle the size of the lid plus twice its depth all around for the lid cover. From the muslin, cut a rectangle the size of the lid for the lining. From the printed fabric, cut a strip the circumference of the box plus 1¼" (3 cm) × the height of the box plus 1⅝" (4 cm), and a rectangle the size of the box's base plus ¼" (5 mm) all around for the base. Paint the inside of the lid and box.

1 With an erasable marker, draw a simple design centrally on the lid cover to echo the printed fabric and featuring motifs to be outlined and stuffed. With wrong sides facing, baste the lining centrally to the lid cover.

2 Place the fabric in a hoop. Using two strands of embroidery floss, backstitch along the lines of the motifs. If you like, use other embroidery stitches to fill in accompanying shapes. Here, the leaf shapes are filled with satin stitch.

3 Cut small slits in the lining behind the trapunto motifs, taking care not to cut the top surface.

4 Using a crochet hook, insert batting into the motifs then overcast stitch the slits closed. Trim the lining, leaving ¼"

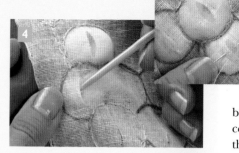

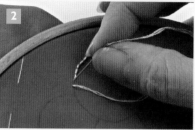
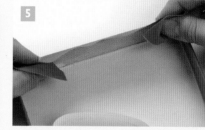

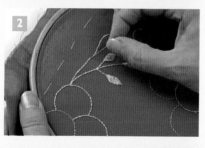

(5 mm) to the edges of the cover. Remove the basting.

5 Apply double sided tape just inside the lid rim; peel off the backing. Place the lid face down on the center of the lid lining. Stick the long then the short fabric edges smoothly inside the rim, folding under the fullness at the corners.

6 Check the fabric and, if necessary, adjust so it lays taut and smooth by resticking it to the tape. Apply tape to a length of ribbon. Trim the tape to the ribbon's width. Stick the ribbon over the raw fabric edges inside the lid cover. Cut off the excess ribbon.

7 Press under ⅝" (1.5 cm) at one end of the printed fabric strip. Wrap the strip around the box with 1" (2.5 cm) extending above the box. Stick the short raw edge to the box with double sided tape. Lap the pressed edge over the short raw edge and tape in place.

8 Tape the upper edge inside the box. Cover the raw edge with ribbon as before. Tape the lower edges under the box. Fold under the fabric base ¼" (5 mm) on all sides, press, and baste. Slipstitch the fabric base all around the lower edge of the box. Remove basting.

Corded quilting

This form of raised quilting, which can be done by hand or machine, involves stitching parallel lines, about $\frac{1}{4}$" (6 mm) apart on to a double layer of fabric to create channels into which a filling is inserted. The filling is inserted from the wrong side and afterward, unless the motif is applied to another fabric, the quilting is lined to hide any filling that shows and prevent it raveling.

Corded quilting is best worked on a closely woven fabric with a sheen such as satin, silk jersey, or polished cotton. For the backing, use a loosely woven fabric such as cheesecloth, through which the cord can be inserted easily. Make sure the material is pre-shrunk and dye-fast. Use a contrasting colored thread for the basting and a matching thread for your main fabric.

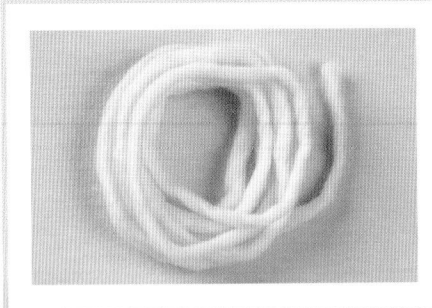

FILLING

Use a thick yarn — wool, pearl cotton, or cotton cord are all suitable. Make sure it is pre-shrunk and if colored, dye-fast.

BASIC CORDED METHOD

1 Transfer your design to the right side of the top fabric (see page 15). Always use a hoop to ensure an even tension. With wrong sides facing and the material held in a hoop, baste the top and bottom fabric pieces together. Using neat running stitches, stitch along the lines of the design. Once the fabrics are joined, remove the basting stitches and the hoop.

2 Thread a blunt-ended number 16 or 18 tapestry needle with a length of yarn sufficient for your design and make a small entry hole in the backing fabric.

3 Work the thread through the hole and along the channels of your design, leaving a ¼" (5 mm) tail at the opening. Bring out the needle through the backing approximately 1¼" (3 cm) from the opening.

4 Reinsert the needle through the same gap and continue to thread cord through the channels, taking it out at 1¼" (3 cm) intervals. On curves and corners, bring the needle out in the same way but leave a little loop of cord showing to prevent the

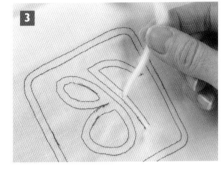

fabric puckering. When finished, clip the cord, leaving a ¼" (5 mm) tail.

5 When channels cross, cut the cord, leaving a ¼" (5 mm) tail. Re-insert your needle on the other side of the channel, leaving another ¼" (5 mm) tail.

UNBACKED VARIATION

If you are going to apply a raised motif to another fabric, you don't have to work with a backing fabric. Simply transfer your design onto the wrong side of your top fabric and secure filling along the lines using a matching thread.

MACHINE SEWING

If using a machine for corded quilting, place wrong sides facing and baste both fabrics together using basting thread. Then stitch with matching thread, following the design lines, using straight stitches of a medium length. Remove basting thread.

This pillow, with its crown motif of corded quilting, is fit for queen! The cover is removable and can be laundered with care.

You will need

- 1 yard (90 cm) fabric

- Remnant for lining

- Rectangular cushion form 12" × 16" (30 × 40 cm)

- Matching thread

- Filling

You can apply a motif to a store-bought pillowcase with appliqué (see pages 78 and 80) or make it integral to the case, as shown below.

MAKING THE PILLOW

Cut out two pieces of fabric 14" × 18" (35 × 45 cm) – this is the front panel on which you will create your design. Cut out another piece of fabric 14" × 26" (35 × 65 cm) for the back panel. Fold the back panel into thirds widthwise and press. Cut along one of the folds to produce two pieces – the larger one should be twice the size of the smaller. Mark the cut edges with pins.

1 Enlarge the motif as necessary and transfer it (see page 15) to the wrong side of the front piece of your fabric.

2 Baste the backing piece to the front and then stitch along both sides of the marked lines on the design to create channels ¼" (5 mm) apart.

3 Insert the cord as directed on page 37. Carefully slipstitch a lining to the backing piece to cover the cording.

4 Now take your two back pieces and turn under each of the marked edges ¼" (5 mm), then 1½" (4 cm) and press. Pin and topstitch both hems in place.

5 Pin the back pieces to the front, right sides together, matching raw edges and making sure the hemmed edges overlap. Stitch around the sides, ⅝" (1.5 cm) in

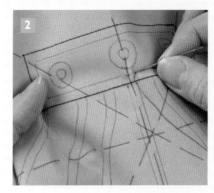

from the edge. Stitch a second line of stitching just inside the first at the side where the back panels overlap, for extra strength. Snip across each corner to reduce the bulk and make a neater finish.

6 Finish the raw edges with zig-zag stitch to neaten and prevent fraying. Turn the cushion cover to the right side through the opening and press, being careful not to flatten the crown. Carefully stitch all around the case, 1½" (4 cm) in from the edge through all fabric layers, to create a flange. Insert the cushion form.

TEMPLATE

Simple and quick, this is an easy method to join layers of fabric while still producing an attractive finish.

Particularly effective when making items that have a thick layer of batting, tied quilting is worked by making a series of double knots through all three layers to secure the layers. If the quilt is tied on the back, the ties will be virtually invisible on the front, leaving only small indentations that can form an attractive pattern of their own.

Alternatively, if you wish to make the ties a decorative feature, tie the quilt on the front so that the ends are visible, or use a contrasting color thread to make them stand out from the background.

MAKING TIES

Ties must be spaced every 2½"
(6 cm) if you are using polyester
batting, and closer if using cotton
batting. You can use silk or cotton
thread, embroidery floss, or yarn for
the ties. Work with a crewel needle
and an 18" to 24" (45 to 60 cm)
length of your chosen thread.

SEPARATE TIES

1 Assemble the the layers as
directed on page 11. Decide on
where you wish the ends of the ties to
show, and work from that side of the
piece. Leaving a short end of thread,
make a backstitch through all 3
layers.

2 Make another backstitch in the
same spot and cut the thread, leaving
a short end.

3 Tie the ends together in a double
knot. Trim the ends evenly. Continue
tying knots across the item, spacing
them evenly.

JOINED TIES

1 If the ties are going to be spaced
close together, work two backstitches,
then go on to the next area without
cutting the thread. Continue with the
same length of thread until you run out.

2 Cut the thread in between the ties,
then tie the ends into a double knot.

Top a simple wicker basket with a neat cover that not only looks good but also will keep insects off the contents. Here, a spotted furnishing fabric is tied to a backing with large contrasting buttons and embroidery floss. A striped ribbon secures it to the basket.

You will need

For a basket 15½" (40 cm) long and 12½" (32 cm) wide

- Fabric, batting, and lining: ⅔ yard (60 cm) of any width fabric

- ⅔ yard (60 cm) bias binding, ½" (1 cm) wide

- 2 yards (1.8 m) bias binding,, ¾" (2 cm) wide

- Seven 1¼" (3 cm) diameter buttons

- Stranded cotton embroidery floss

- Crewel embroidery needle

- 3¼ yards (3 m) striped ribbon, ⅝" (1.5 cm) wide

- Bodkin

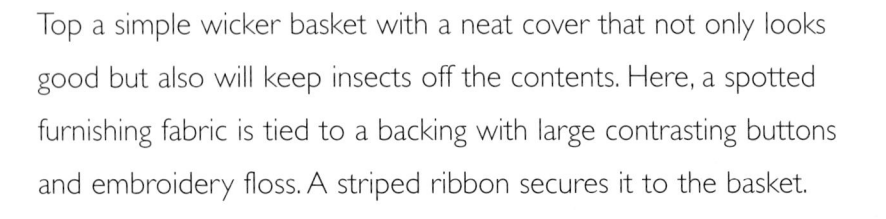

43 | MAKING THE COVER

Cut a rectangle of paper to the same length and width of your basket.

1 Tape the paper to the top of the basket with masking tape. Cut slits in the paper around the handles so that the paper lays flat. On the paper, draw a smoothly curved edge around the handles. Draw any curves on the basket's circumference, at the corners, for example.

2 Remove the paper and cut along the curved lines. Draw around the cut paper on another piece to make the final pattern. Add 2¼"(5.5 cm) to the outer edges and ⅜" (8 mm) to the handle cut-outs.

3 Cut out the pattern. Use the pattern to cut the cover, batting, and lining.

4 Place the batting between the fabric and lining and baste. With right sides facing, pin ½" (1 cm) wide bias binding to the handle cut-outs. Stitch the binding, making ¼"(5 mm) seam allowance. Trim away the batting in the seam allowance. Clip the curves. Press the binding to the underside and slipstitch in place to the lining. Topstitch close to the handle cut-outs.

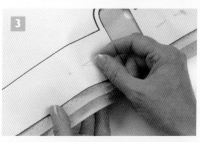

5 With right sides facing, stitch ¾" (2 cm) wide bias binding to the outer edges of the basket cover with the binding extending ⅜" (8 mm) beyond the handle cut-outs and making ⅜" (8 mm) seam allowance. Trim away the batting in the seam allowance. Clip the curves and trim the seam allowance to ¼" (5 mm). Turn under the extending ends of the binding and handsew to the binding.

6 Turn the binding to the underside. To make the drawstring channel, pin the binding to the lining, folding any fullness at the corners in small pleats.

7 Baste close to the inner edge of the binding. On the right side, topstitch close to the outer edges of the cover and along the basting. Remove the basting.

8 Thread a crewel needle with a double length of six strands of embroidery floss. Make a tie at the center of the cover (see page 41), threading on a button before tying the threads on top. Arrange the remaining buttons equally around the center button and tie them to the cover. Scatter additional floss ties among them.

9 Cut the ribbon in half. Thread each piece through a channel using a bodkin. Slip the cover over the basket and tie the ribbons in a bow below the handles.

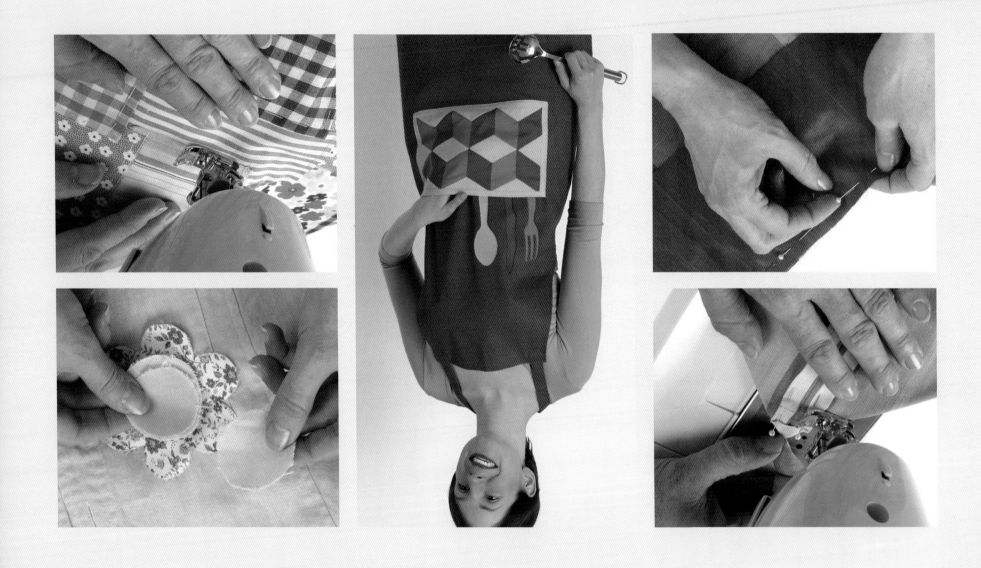

PATCHWORK AND APPLIQUÉ

Joining differently patterned fabrics together or applying them to background fabrics can result in exciting soft furnishings and fashionable garments. Here, you will find all the techniques necessary to piece fabrics by hand or machine and recreate traditional patchwork patterns that have stood the test of time. You also will discover how easy it is to apply designs as hand or machine appliqués to enliven existing items. Finally, the thirteen exciting projects on offer allow you to use these traditional techniques to produce some envy-inducing contemporary garments and accessories.

Templates

Patchwork designs depend on templates for their creation. These are used for cutting out the individual pieces. Ready-made templates are widely available but it is easy to make your own. Trace patterns from a book, magazine, or other source, or draw your own design on graph paper.

READY-MADE TEMPLATES

A wide range of shapes are available in plastic or metal, which will be more durable than home-made ones. Plastic and window templates can be positioned on the fabric to create special effects. Window templates provide for the seam allowance; other types do not.

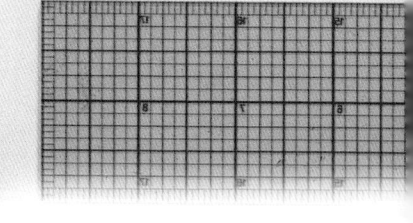

Marking tools
Use a dressmaker's pencil for all types of fabric.

Template material
Medium-weight cardboard and plastic can be used. Graph paper can be glued to the template to aid cutting.

Cutting tools
A craft knife will cut through cardboard or plastic. Use a metal-edge ruler and cutting mat.

Temporary adhesive
Use this for sticking paper templates to cardboard and for securing appliqué pieces temporarily to base fabric.

Measuring equipment
Use a transparent plastic ruler to mark out seam allowances and templates, and a compass for drafting curved templates.

MAKING TEMPLATES

Accuracy is very important so make sure you measure carefully and use sharpened dressmaker's pencils to draw the lines. For machine sewing templates or window templates you will need to add a ¼" (5 mm) seam allowance all around each pattern piece. Label the pieces with letters and the pattern name, then draw a grain line (see page 9).

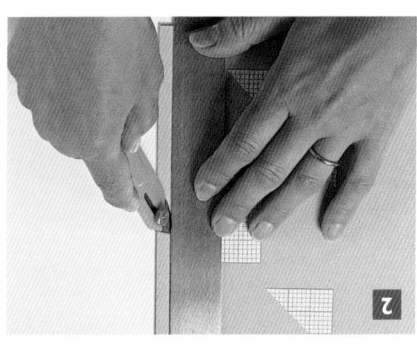

1 Cut out your paper pieces and spray the wrong side with temporary adhesive. Leaving ½" (1 cm) between pieces, press on to a sheet of medium-weight cardboard or clear acetate.

2 Place the cardboard or acetate on a cutting mat or stack of newspapers and use a craft knife and a metal-edge ruler to cut out the templates – either along the edge of the paper or along the marked seamline.

3 For complicated or curved designs, mark notches in the edges of the templates to aid in matching the pieces when you sew them together. Cut out notches using the knife.

CUTTING OUT FABRIC PIECES

Mark the seamline and cutting lines on the wrong side of the fabric if you are hand sewing. Mark just the outer cutting line if you are machine sewing. As a general rule, mark the longest edge of a patchwork piece along the fabric grain (see page 9).

FOR HAND SEWING

1 Position the pieces at least ½" (1 cm) apart when marking them on fabric.

2 Either mark the cutting lines, or judge by eye, and cut the pieces apart.

FOR MACHINE SEWING

When marking the shapes on fabric, position pieces with edges touching.

Hand sewing is more time consuming than machine but produces a unique look. Always sew pieces with the right sides of the fabric together and the raw edges exactly even with each other. Stitches must be evenly spaced, and not too crowded. Seam allowances are ¼" (5 mm) wide and must be marked on the patches when sewing by hand.

SETTING IN

This is done when you have to sew a piece into an angle formed by other joined pieces. When sewing the initial pieces, end your stitching ¼" (5 mm) from the edge. Backstitch or knot the end. Mark a dot on the corner of the piece to be inset to show the position of the corner.

1 Pin the patch to be inset into the angle with right sides together; match the dot to the corner. Stitch seam from the outer edge toward the center. Make a backstitch at the central dot.

2 Swing the adjacent edge of the patch to align it with the other edge of the angled piece, then continue stitching the adjacent seam, backstitching at the end.

Baste the pieces together to secure before sewing them together using light colored thread that will contrast with the fabric. For the final stitching, work with 18" (45 cm) lengths of matching thread knotted at the end.

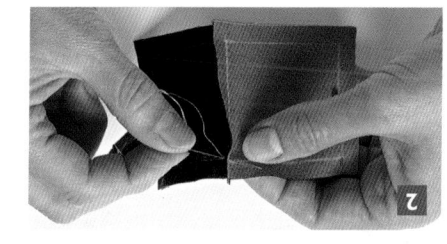

1 Hold the fabric so that you can see the sewing lines on each side. Make two backstitches at the beginning of the seam and work evenly spaced running stitches from corner to corner along the marked seam lines.

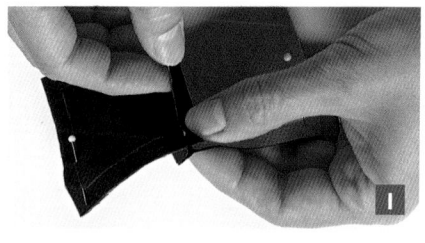

2 Check your stitching to ensure that it is exactly on the marked lines, front and back. Make two backstitches at the opposite corner.

JOINING ROWS

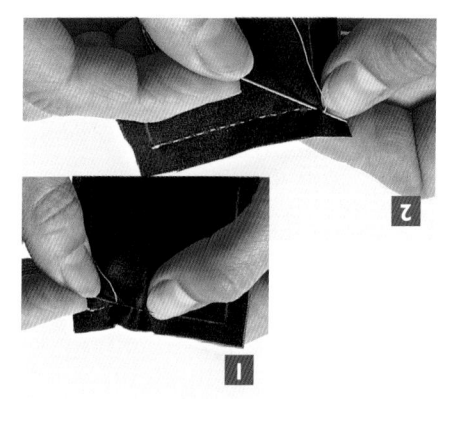

1 Hold the sewn pieces together with the right sides facing, matching the seams carefully, and inserting pins where necessary to secure the pieces.

2 At each seam, knot or backstitch the thread, then insert needle through the seam allowance to the other side so that you are leaving seam allowances free. Knot or backstitch again before sewing the rest of the seam.

SEWING OVER PAPERS

1 Using the outer edge of a window template, cut out fabric pieces. Use the inner edge to cut out papers. Center a paper on wrong side of a fabric piece, then pin. Fold one seam allowance over paper without creasing it; baste one stitch through fabric and paper, leaving tail of thread free and unknotted.

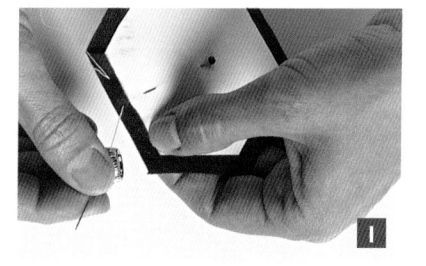

2 Fold adjacent seam allowance over paper, forming a sharp corner. Baste over corner to secure, bringing needle up in middle of next seam allowance. Repeat for remaining edges. Cut thread, leaving end free. Remove pin. Press gently and repeat for other patches.

3 To join, place pieces with right sides facing, matching the corners. Whipstitch the edges together from corner to corner, backstitching at each end. Do not sew in papers. Removing basting stitches and papers. Gently press finished work.

To save time, many quilters use a machine to join together patchwork pieces. Always use a seam allowance of ¼" (5 mm). Before joining the patchwork pieces, test the sewing machine's tension by stitching on a fabric scrap. When you have to sew a piece into an angle formed by other joined pieces, use setting in.

PRESSING

Always press seam allowances to one side to make the seams stronger. Press every piece before it is crossed by another. Always press intersecting seam allowances in opposite directions. After joining, press the new seam allowance toward darker fabric.

SEAM RIPPER

If stitches cause the fabric to pucker, remove them carefully using a seam ripper. Cut through every third or fourth stitch on one side. On the opposite side, pull the thread – it should lift away easily.

PIECING BY MACHINE

When machine sewing, use a standard straight stitch at 10 to 12 stitches per inch (2.5 cm). The edge of the presser foot or a line on the throat plate of the sewing machine should be used as a stitching guide.

1 Hold the patches together; pin, if necessary. Place the edge of the patches beneath the presser foot. Lower it and needle into the edge of the fabric. Stitch forward slowly, guiding the fabric with your hand. At the end of the seam, pull out a length of thread and break it.

2 Backstitch to secure stitches, using reverse lever on sewing machine, or make stitches tiny. It isn't necessary to backstitch at each edge of each patch – only where you know that a seam or edge will be under stress, or when insetting (see opposite).

3 Patches can be sewed together in a chain to save time and thread. Feed each new set of patches beneath presser foot. Feed dogs will draw them beneath needle. Cut chain apart with scissors after sewing, and press seam allowances.

JOINING ROWS

Press the matching seam allowances in opposite directions to reduce bulk and to make matching the seam easier. Pin the pieces together directly through the stitching, and to the right and left of the seam to prevent the pieces from shifting as you sew.

SETTING IN

1 Pin the patch to be inset into the angle with right sides together. Stitch the seam from the center toward the outer edge. Break the thread.

2 Swing the adjacent angled piece to the other edge of the patch and pin. Stitch from the center to the outer edge. There should be no puckers on the right side of the work. Clip off any threads. Press carefully.

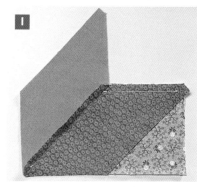

The seams are carefully matched at the corners

BABY BLOCKS APRON

Embellish a ready-made apron with a smart patchwork pocket made using a classic shape. If you like, you can add appliquéd utensils. The diamond shaped patches used for the blocks create a three-dimensional look.

You will need

• Fabric apron

• ⅓ yard (30 cm) fabric in color A, 36" (90 cm) wide

• ⅛ yard (12 cm) fabric in colors B and C, each 36" (90 cm) wide

• ¼ yard (23 cm) lining fabric 60" (150 cm) wide

• 2 yards (1 m 80 cm) bias binding

• Bonding web

• Erasable marker

If necessary, unpick any pockets on the apron and discard them.

1 Use the template to cut six diamonds each from fabrics A, B, and C. Cut four of the C fabric diamonds in half along the solid line and two diamonds in half along the broken lines. Cut one A fabric diamond and one B fabric diamond in half along the broken lines. Refer to the photo to position the patches right sides up.

2 Stitch the patches together making a ¼" (5 mm) seam allowance to make the pocket (see the setting in technique on page 51).

3 Trim the raw edges of the pocket level. Cut the lining fabric to the size of the pocket and pin and baste the lining to the pocket. Bind the side and bottom edges of the pocket with ready-made bias binding (see page 21); slipstitch in place on the underside of the pocket. Stitch bias binding to the upper straight edge of the pocket, having ½" (1 cm) of the binding extending beyond the ends of the bound edges. Turn in the ends and slipstitch in place.

4 Using the templates, enlarged as required, cut out the knife, fork, and spoon from your fabrics. Attach to the apron with bonding web, following the manufacturer's instructions. Zig-zag stitch around each item with matching thread.

5 Carefully pin the patchwork pocket to the apron.

6 Topstitch using matching thread along the side and bottom edges, just inside the bias binding.

TEMPLATES

2½" (6.25 cm)

¼ inch (5 mm) allowance

8½" (21.25 cm)

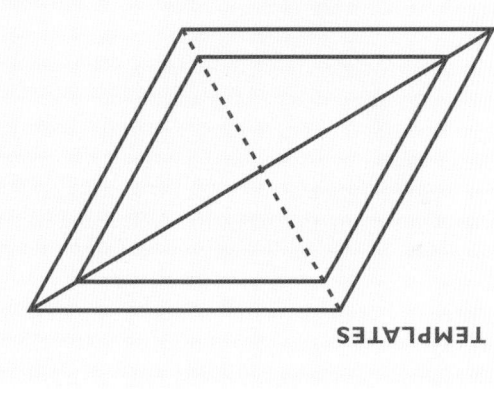

Patchwork blocks

Patterns are made up of a number of different pieces, known as patches, and described as 4, 8, or 9 patch. Sets of templates for particular designs are widely available, or you can buy individual ones, or make your own. Blocks are assembled in sections, starting with the smallest pieces and building outward.

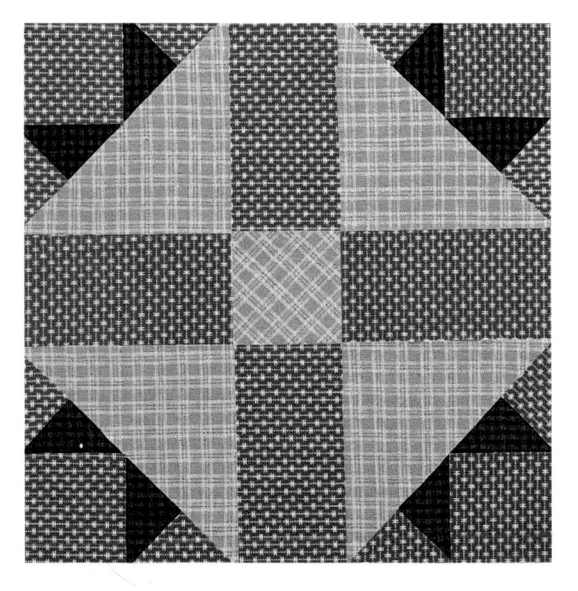

The top of this cushion, made in the cross and crown pattern, consists of one 9 patch block, where the four corner patches are pieced.

CROSS AND CROWN

To make one 9 patch block with four corner patches consisting of pieces requires five templates and 29 fabric pieces: eight bright and eight dark A; four bright B, four light C; four bright D, and one E.

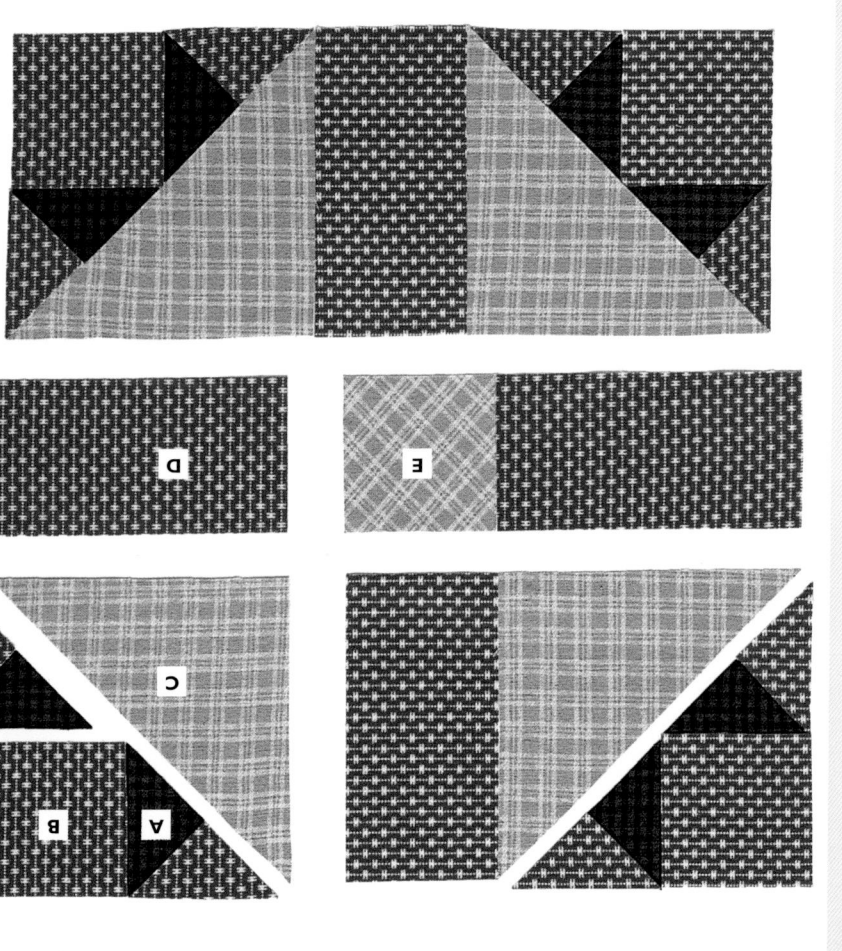

EIGHT SEAM JOIN

Complex seams and joins are a feature of certain types of designs. Here, eight diamond shapes need to meet accurately at a center point, whose bulk has to be reduced by careful stitching and pressing.

1 Sew the diamonds together, beginning and ending the seam with backstitches ¼" (5 mm) from the edges. Sew 2 pairs of diamonds together to form each half of the design.

2 Insert a pin through the point of the center diamond on the wrong side of one piece, ¼" (5 mm) away from the edge to be joined. The same pin should be inserted through the right side of the other piece at same point.

3 Pin the remainder of the seam, then stitch carefully. Press from the wrong side, opening up the seam allowance around the center point to reduce the bulk.

This contemporary patchwork bag is constructed from rectangles of plain and patterned fabrics. An appliquéd seagull is a fun decorative touch which can be outlined with embroidery floss and finished with a tiny button or bead. Cord makes an easy to fit and attractive adjustable handle.

You will need

- ½ yard (45 cm) plain fabric A, 36" (90 cm) wide

- ¼ yard (23 cm) denim fabric B, 36" (90 cm) wide

- ½ yard (45 cm) striped fabric C, 36" (90 cm) wide

- 8" (20 cm) square fabric in turquoise for motif

- Four ⅝" (1.5 cm) metal eyelets

- 2 yards (1.8 m) cord, 1" (2.5 cm) wide

- Stranded cotton embroidery floss

- Small button

MAKING THE SHOPPER

From fabric A, cut out two rectangles 17" × 6¼"(43 × 16 cm) for bands and one rectangle 17" × 34¾" (43 × 87 cm) for the lining. From fabric B, cut out two rectangles 17" × 6¼" (43 × 16 cm) for bands. From fabric C, cut out one rectangle 17" × 13½" (43 × 35 cm) for bands and base.

Note: use ⅝" (1.5 cm) allowance for all seams.

1 Stitch band A to band B along the long edges. Repeat with another A and B. Press the seams toward A.

2 Stitch band C to bands B along the long edge. Press the seams toward B.

3 Enlarge the seagull template and use to cut out shape from turquoise fabric. Place motif left of center on the front; pin in place. Turn edge under ¼"(5 cm) and using 2 strands of floss, secure with small neat stitches near the edge. Add the button.

4 With right sides facing and matching side edges, stitch side seams of front and back. Press the seams open.

5 Mark along the fold at the base of the shopper with pins. Match the pins to one

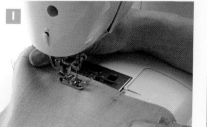

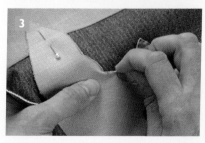

side seam with the right sides facing. Pin at right angles across the seam, 2" (5 cm) from the end of the seam. Stitch as pinned. Trim the seam to seam allowance. Repeat on the other side seam to form the shopper's base.

6 Fold lining lengthwise in half. Stitch down both sides. Finish bottom as in step 5 above. With wrong side facing out, place in bag. Turn under the tops of the lining and bag by ⅝" (1.5 cm) and top stitch close to the edge on the front.

7 Fix the metal eyelets to the bag, 4¾" (12 cm) in from the side seams. Thread the cord through and make double knots under the eyelets.

TEMPLATE

← 6" (15 cm) →
¼" (5 mm) allowance

PATCHWORK PET CUSHION

Reward a loyal pet with this super cushion on which it
will be delighted to relax. The cushion is 24" (60 cm)
square and features paving stone patchwork blocks made
up of plain colors and an animal print.

You will need

• 1¼ yards (1.2 m) fabric B, 36" (90 cm) wide

• ¼ yard (23 cm) fabric A, 36" (90 cm) wide

• ⅔ yard (60 cm) fabric C, 36" (90 cm) wide

• 24" (60 cm) square cushion pad

MAKING THE CUSHION

From fabric A, cut out four 7"(17.5 cm) squares. From fabric B, cut out four 6½" (16.5 cm) squares for the front, one 25" (62.5 cm) square for the back and two 25" × 16" (62.5 × 40 cm) rectangles for the back panels. Cut out four 9½" (23 cm) squares of fabric C. Cut the B and C squares diagonally into halves.

Note: Stitch the seams making ⅝" (1.5 cm) seam allowance and stitch the seams with right sides facing.

1 To make one block, stitch the long edge of four B triangles to each edge of square A. Press the seams toward the B triangles.

2 Stitch the long edge of four C triangles to one edge of the stitched B triangles. Press the seams toward the C triangles.

3 Make up three more blocks in the same way. Join the blocks together to form a large square for the cushion front.

4 Turn under ¼" (5 mm) then 1½" (4 cm) on one long edge of each back panel and press in place to form a hem. Stitch close to the inner pressed edges.

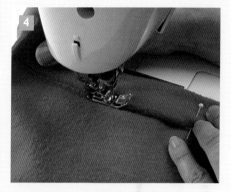

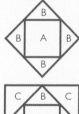

5 Pin the back panels to the front with right sides facing, matching the raw edges and overlapping the hems at the center. Stitch the outer edges. Stitch again just inside the first stitching for extra strength.

6 Clip the corners and trim off excess seam allowance. Turn right side out and insert the cushion pad.

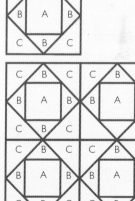

TEMPLATES

| # BACKED THROW

This cosy throw is actually a single giant star block. The throw measures 72" (180 cm) square. It is backed and padded for extra warmth and the edges of the backing are brought to the front to bind the edges. The layers are tied with felt circles. If you intend to wash the throw, use felted wool for the circles. Traditional craft felts need to be dry cleaned.

You will need

- ½ yard (45 cm) fabric A, 60" (150 cm) wide

- ½ yard (45 cm) fabric B, 60" (150 cm) wide

- ½ yard (45 cm) fabric C, 60" (150 cm) wide

- 5¾ yards (5.2 m) fabric D, 60" (150 cm) wide

- 4¼ yards (3.9 m) batting or

- curtain interlining, 60" (150 cm) wide

- 9" (23 cm) felt square

- Coton a broderie embroidery yarn

- Thick needle

- Matching sewing thread

TEMPLATE

MAKING THE THROW

From fabric A, cut four 12½" (32 cm) squares. From fabric B, cut two 18" (45 cm) squares. Cut the A and B squares diagonally in half. From fabric C, cut four 12½" (32 cm) squares for the corner squares. From fabric D, cut one 24½" (61 cm) square for the center square; two 48½" × 12¼" (121 × 30.5 cm) strips and two 72" × 12¼" (180 × 30.5 cm) strips, and two 76" × 38¼" (190 × 95.6 cm) rectangles for the backing. From the batting, cut two 76" × 38¼" (190 × 96 cm) rectangles. From the felt, cut twelve 1⅜" (3.5 cm) circles.

Stitch the block making ¼" (5 mm) seam allowances and stitch the seams with right sides facing.

1 Stitch the long edge of one triangle A to one short edge of each triangle B. Press the seams toward triangle A. Join another triangle A to the other short edge of triangle B and press the seams toward triangle A.

2 Set two of the pieced triangles aside. On the remaining pieced triangles, stitch the short edges of triangle A to one edge of square C to make two stitched strips.

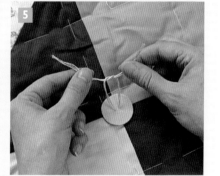

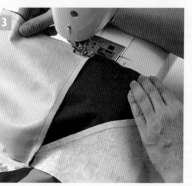

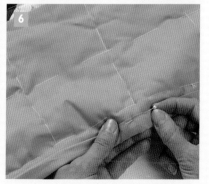

3 Stitch the set-aside pieced triangles to the two vertical opposite edges of square D. Stitch the stitched strips from step 2 to the horizontal edges of square D.

4 Stitch each short strip D to two opposite edges of the patchwork. Stitch the long strip Ds to the adjacent edges. Stitch the backing rectangles together to form a square. Using overcasting, stitch the batting rectangles with the long edges butted together. Assemble the throw, see page 11.

5 Pin a felt circle to the seam of square D at each adjoining seam and to the outer corners of square Cs. Tie the layers together through the middle of the circles using six strands of embroidery yarn, see page 41.

6 Stitch close to the outer edges of strip Ds. Trim the edges of the batting to match the throw. Trim the backing 1½" (4 cm) beyond the edges of the block. Press under ½" (1 cm) on the edges of the backing. Fold the backing over the outer edges of the block. Slipstitch the pressed edges to the throw.

| Log cabin patchwork

This patchwork technique involves sewing strips of fabric around a central shape to produce a variety of effects; you don't need any templates but rotary cutting simplifies the cutting process. It is essential that you work with strongly contrasting fabrics so one half of the block is light and the other half is dark. To construct the block, begin in the middle with a square and add strips in a counter-clockwise direction.

CONSTRUCTING A BLOCK

1 Cut strips to desired width with a ½" (1 cm) seam allowance – making sure to cut across the entire width of fabric. Cut a square for the center.

2 With right sides facing, place the square against a light strip, matching the edges. Stitch, then cut the strip even with the square. Press the seam allowance toward the center.

3 Choose a different light fabric for the second strip and sew to the pieced center, trimming away the excess fabric so it is even with the center. Press lightly.

4 Pick a dark fabric for the third strip. Continuing counter-clockwise, sew the pieced center to the strip, trimming away the excess fabric so it is even with the center. Press lightly.

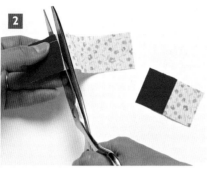

5 Select a different dark fabric for the fourth strip. Sew to the pieced center, trimming away the excess fabric as before. Press lightly.

6 Continue working counter-clockwise, adding two light strips, then two dark strips around the center. Don't place the same fabrics next to each other. Trim the strips and press lightly after each addition.

LOG CABIN ALBUM COVER

Although quilting and patchwork are usually associated with more utilitarian fabrics, silk dupion works to great effect and is economical to use on a small item such as this slip-on cover in a traditional design.

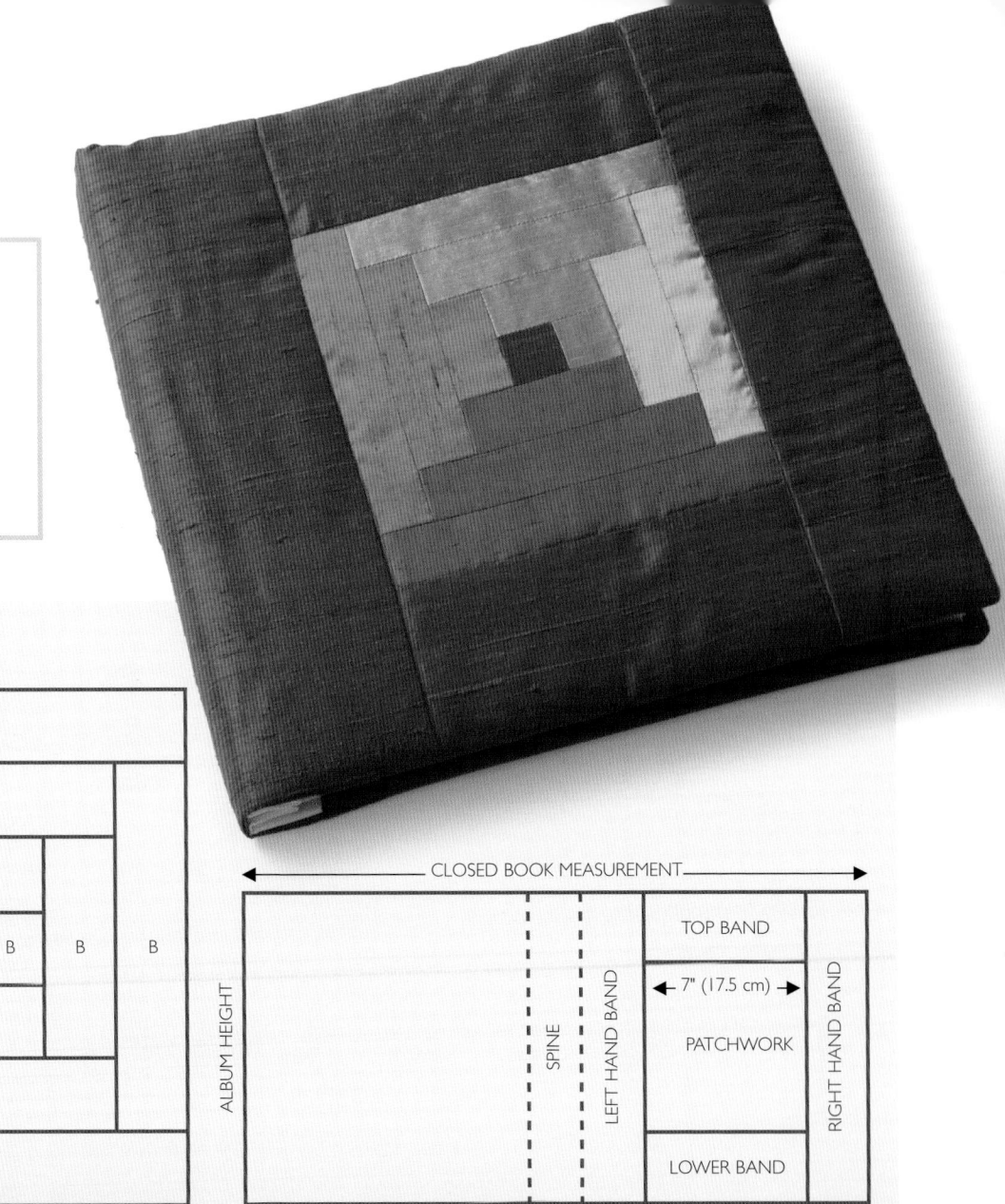

You will need

- 36" (90 cm) wide silk dupion in color A; for amount see below

- ⅛ yard (12 cm) silk dupion 36" (90 cm) wide in colors B and C

- Album, at least 7" (17.5 cm) wide and high

- 44" (112 cm) wide lining; for amount see below

- 2 oz. batting; for amount see below

- Matching sewing thread

TEMPLATE

| B |
| B |
| B |
| C C C | A | B | B | B |
| C |
| C |
| C |

7" (17.5 cm)

CLOSED BOOK MEASUREMENT

ALBUM HEIGHT

SPINE

LEFT HAND BAND

TOP BAND

7" (17.5 cm)

PATCHWORK

RIGHT HAND BAND

LOWER BAND

BACK

FRONT

For the patchwork, cut out a 1½" (4 cm) square of fabric A for the center. Cut out one 1½" (4 cm) strip across the width of fabrics B and C.

Measure the height of the album. Next, measure the closed book around the cover and spine from opening edge to opening edge. Make a note of the depth of the spine and the width of the front and back cover (when added together, they should be the same measurement as the closed book measurement). On scrap paper, refer to the diagram to draw the album. Draw a 7" (17.5 cm) square in the center front for the patchwork.

From fabric A, cut out all the album pieces adding a ½" (1 cm) seam allowance to all edges. Cut out two strips for the top and lower bands and cut out one strip for the right hand band. Cut out a rectangle for the album back that is the album height times the width of the back plus the spine plus the left hand band.

Cut out a rectangle of lining and batting that is the same size as the closed book measurement plus the seam allowance times the album height plus the seam allowance. Cut out two facings from fabric A that are the front measurement

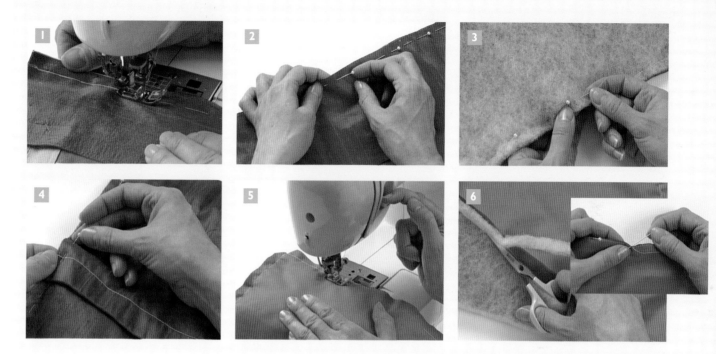

times the album height plus the seam allowance.

1 See pages 62-3 to make the log cabin patchwork. Make sure to use ¼" (5 mm) seam allowances. With right sides facing, stitch the top and lower bands to the top and lower edges of the patchwork. Press the seams toward the bands.

2 With right sides facing, stitch the right hand band to the right hand edge and the back cover to the left hand edge

of the patchwork. Press the seams away from the patchwork.

3 Baste the batting to the wrong side of the cover. Stitch in the ditch (see page 19) along the band seams and outer edge of the patchwork.

4 Stitch a 1" (2.5 cm) double hem on one "album height" edge of the facings. With right sides facing, pin the facings to the opening edges of the cover, matching the raw edges.

5 With right sides facing, pin and baste the lining and cover together. Stitch the outer edges together leaving a gap to turn through in the lower edge.

6 Clip the corners and carefully trim away the batting in the seam allowance. Turn right side out, turn the facings to the inside. Press the cover and slipstitch the opening closed. Slip the cover on to the album.

Also known as openwork patchwork, this requires a circular template. If not applied to a background fabric, the puffs create a lace-like effect. Even if stitched to a backing fabric, this type of work cannot be quilted, so it is used purely as decoration.

Check your color scheme by arranging the puffs in color groups. The finished puffs will be about half the size of the cut circles.

CIRCLE TEMPLATES

The best way to make a perfect circle is to use a compass. Make sure your pencil end is sharp and the paper is held securely. Place the tip of the compass on the paper and describe an arc so that the pencil end marks out a full circle. An easy option is to draw around a small plate or cup.

MAKING YO-YOS

1 Cut out circle templates 3" to 6" (7.5 to 15 cm) in diameter out of card or heavy paper. Pin them to the fabric or draw around them directly onto the fabric. Cut out fabric circles.

2 Turn the fabric under ¼" (5 mm) all around and work evenly spaced running stitches ⅛" (3 mm) from the edge using a strong thread firmly secured at one end. Hold the circle right side down and begin the sewing with a couple of back stitches.

3 Gather the edges up by gently but firmly pulling the thread.

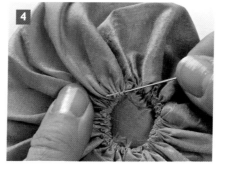

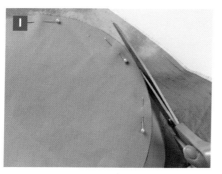

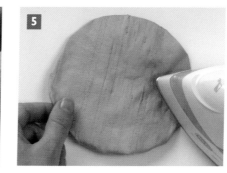

4 Continue pulling until the edges are in the center and form a showercap shape. Then secure the gathering thread with a couple of back stitches.

5 Arrange the gathers so that they are all straight and equally distributed around the circle. Then flatten the puff by pressing it with a warm iron, making sure the folded edges make a well-formed circle. Repeat for all the other puffs.

6 Place the puffs side by side. Where they meet, join with a few overcast stitches. If you don't want a lacy effect, secure the puffs to a suitable backing by stitching around the edges of the patches, while catching some of the ground fabric.

PADDED PUFFS
You can make your puffs more three-dimensional by carefully inserting lightweight batting after step 4. Alternatively, cut a disk of batting the finished diameter and insert before gathering up the edges (step 3).

This round cushion is decorated with a set of eye-catching yo-yos and edged with a box pleated frill. Choose lightweight fabric for the yo-yos so that they will gather easily. Round, feather-filled cushion pads with a deep gusset between the front and back are available to insert into the cushion cover. Making the cover slightly smaller than the cushion makes for a snugger fit.

You will need

- ½ yard (45 cm) lightweight fabric 60" (150 cm) wide for cushion and frill
- ¾ yard (70 cm) lightweight fabric 60" (150 cm) wide for yo-yos
- Velcro®
- 15" (38 cm) diameter round cushion pad
- 7 small self-covering buttons

MAKING THE CUSHION

Cut out a circle of card the size of your cushion pad to use as a template for the front cover. Cut one half circle with an extra 4" (10 cm) width on the straight side to use as a template for the back cover. Cut out a 10" (25 cm) diameter circle of card to use as a template for the yo-yos. From the cushion fabric, cut out one circle for the front and two half circles for the back.

Cut out three 48" × 4¾" (120 × 12 cm) strips for the frill. Cut out seven circles for the yo-yos.

1 Join the frills end to end with right sides facing to make a ring, making ¼" (5 mm) seam allowance. Press the frill lengthwise in half with wrong sides facing. Pin and baste the raw edges together.

2 Starting at a seam, mark the raw edge of the strip at 1" (2.5 cm) intervals with pins. Bring the first two pins together to make a pleat. Pin in place. Bring the next two pleats together in the opposite direction so that the pair of pleats form a box pleat. Pin in place. Continue pinning box pleats along the frill.

3 Making ⅝" (1.5 cm) seam allowance, pin and baste the frill to the circumference of the cushion front with right sides facing. If necessary, adjust the depth of a few pleats to make the frill fit.

4 On the straight sides of the back pieces (the 4" [10 cm]) extensions, turn under ⅜"(8 mm) then 1½" (4 cm) to form a double hem. Stitch close to the edge. Cut a piece of Velcro® 4" (10 cm) shorter than the back cover. Stitch one side of it to the wrong side of one back cover piece and the other piece of Velcro® to the right side of the other fabric back. Overlap the hems by 2" (5 cm).

5 Pin the front and back pieces together and stitch. Turn the cushion right side out.

6 Make seven yo-yos (see page 67) in the contrasting fabric. Follow the manufacturer's instructions to cover the buttons. Attach a self-covered button to the gathered opening of each yo-yo. Attach the yo-yos to the cushion front with a few stitches for each, with one at the center and the others around it. Insert the cushion pad and close the Velcro®.

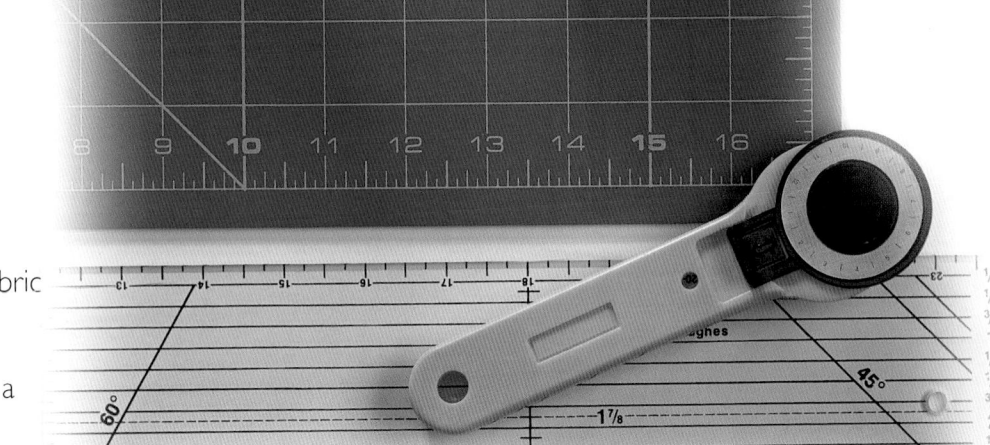

This labor-saving technique enables you to cut through several fabric layers at one time when cutting shapes and also can be used for sashing, borders, and bindings. The necessary implements include a cutting mat with a self-healing surface to grip the fabric; a rotary cutter with a large blade, and a rotary ruler made of clear plastic and marked with straight and angled lines.

SUITABLE PATTERNS

Although most often used to produce the rectangular strips for Log cabin (see page 62) and Seminole patchworks (see page 72), rotary cutting also can be used instead of templates to produce squares, parallelograms, and triangles for other patchwork designs. Patterns can be judged on their difficulty to recreate successfully. The greater the number of pieces, the more difficult the construction due to the number of seams that must be matched. Easy patterns, which have only a few pieces, are best for beginners.

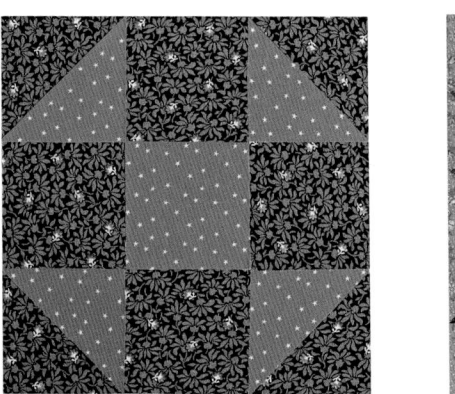

SQUARES AND TRIANGLES
Two shapes and two fabrics are used to create this simple pattern known as Shoo Fly. It is composed of nine squares, four of which are made up of right angle triangles.

LARGE AND SMALL TRIANGLES
Differently sized triangles in five different fabrics are pieced to create Grape Basket. It requires many more seams than Shoo Fly, shown left, and is of medium difficulty.

TRIANGLES, SQUARES, AND PARALLELOGRAMS
As well as an eight-seam join (see page 55), this Diamond Star block of three different shapes requires insetting pieces so is considered difficult.

CUTTING MATERIAL

1 Fold the fabric in half and align the selvages evenly; iron the fabric. If the grain of the fabric is not straight (see page 9), align it before cutting pattern pieces.

2 Place the fabric on the cutting board with the raw edges on the right and the selvages at the top. Place a set square along the straight fold of the fabric. Place the rotary ruler against the left edge of the set square. Remove the set square.

3 Press down firmly on the rotary ruler to prevent shifting. Run the blade of the rotary cutter along the edge of the ruler, keeping the blade upright. Move your hand carefully up the ruler as you cut. Always push the blade away from you.

4 Fold the fabric in half again, aligning the fold with the selvages and matching the cut edges. Using the rotary ruler, measure the desired width of the strip; with the line of the ruler along the cut edge, cut a strip as in step 3.

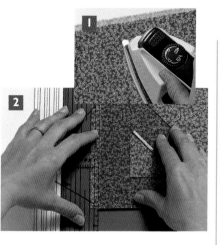

SHAPES

Rotary cutting can produce a variety of straight-edged shapes, thus eliminating the need for many different templates.

TO MAKE SQUARES

Cut a rectangle ½" (1cm) wider than the finished size of the square. Cut off selvages, then place the ruler over the strip and cut a piece to the same width as the strip to create four squares.

TO MAKE HALF-SQUARE TRIANGLES

Cut a strip ⅞" (22 mm) wider than the finished square. Make squares as above; cut in half diagonally.

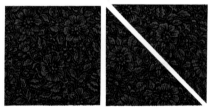

TO MAKE QUARTER-SQUARE TRIANGLES

Use a strip 1¼" (3 cm) larger than the finished long edge. Follow the directions for half-square triangles (above) and then cut in half.

Created by Florida's Seminole Indians, this is a form of strip piecing that is a popular for creating long borders and insertions. Although the finished result looks intricate, the method is not difficult. You will need a rotary cutter, and it is essential that you are accurate when matching and sewing seams.

Pattern I

PATTERN 1

Cut one light ¾" (2 cm) strip, one dark ¾" (2 cm) strip, and two medium 1½" (4 cm) strips. Sew together to make a pieced strip 3" (7.5 cm) wide. Cut the strip into 1½" (4 cm) pieces. Invert one piece and sew both pieces together, matching the seams.

Pattern 2

PATTERN 2

For A, cut two dark 1¾" (4.5 cm) strips, two medium 1¾" (4.5 cm) strips and one bright 1½" (4 cm) strip. Sew together to make a pieced strip 6" (15 cm) wide. For B, cut one dark 3¾" (9.5 cm) strip, one medium 1½" (4 cm) strip, and one dark 1¾" (4.5 cm) strip. Sew together to make a pieced strip 6" (15 cm) wide. Cut the pieced A and B strips into 1½" (4 cm) lengths. Arrange one B piece on each side of an A piece, with one of the B pieces in an inverted position, as shown. Arrange the pieces so that the medium squares line up on each side of the bright square. Sew together, matching the seams.

Invert every alternate B piece in order to complete the pattern sequence.

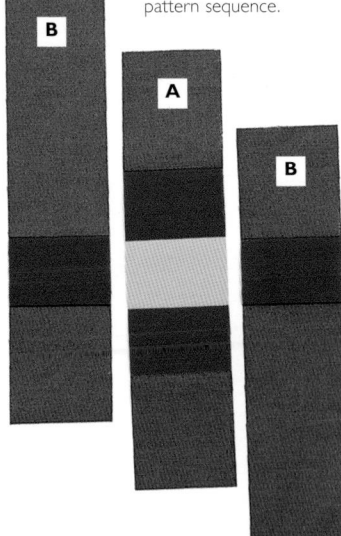

The instructions assume you are working with 45" (112 cm) wide fabric. Cut all the strips across the full width of the fabric, then trim off ½" (1 cm) from the selvage ends, to leave you with a 44" (110 cm) long strip.

1 Using a rotary cutter, cut the required number of strips. For this practice piece, you need three strips — two light, one dark. Coat the strips lightly with spray starch to make them easier to handle, and press. Sew the strips together. Press the seam allowances toward the darker fabrics.

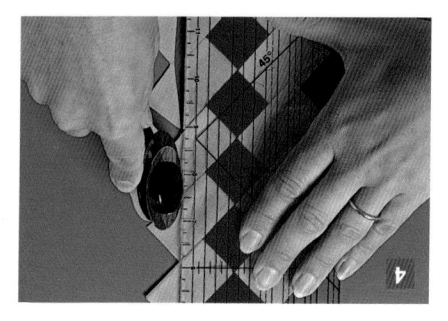

2 Cut the strips into pieces of the required width (here, 1" [2.5 cm]), and arrange on your cutting mat as shown.

3 Sew the pieces together. For another pattern, you may have to alternate or offset the pieces. Press the strip carefully.

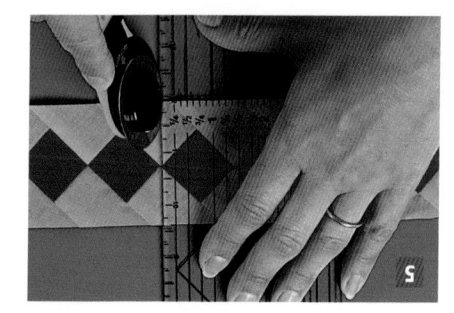

4 Use a rotary cutter to trim the top and bottom edges evenly, if necessary. Remember to leave a ¼" (5 mm) seam allowance all around.

5 You can straighten the angled ends of a Seminole patchwork by making a straight cut through the patchwork. If you have seams that do not quite match, make your cut through this area.

6 Re-arrange the pieces, aligning the diagonal edges. Sew these edges together, matching the seams carefully.

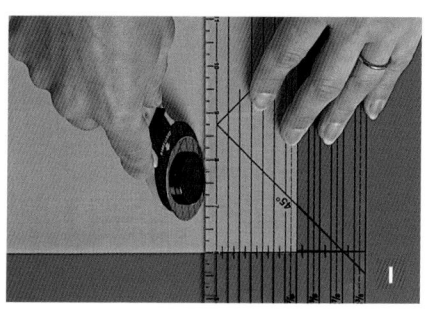

Adding a bright patchwork border to a length of plain fabric creates a handy coverup for the beach. Match one of the border colors, like we did here, to your swimsuit for the best effect. Make sure to prewash all your fabrics before sewing to prevent them shrinking when washed.

You will need

- 2 yards (1.8 m) cotton or poly-cotton fabric in main color, 36" (90 cm) wide

- Short lengths of cotton or poly-cotton fabric in two contrasting colors, 36" (90 cm) wide

- Matching sewing thread

To wear the sarong, wrapped around waist or hips. either tie the top two corners together, or fold over the waistband to secure the fabric in place.

MAKING UP

For the main part of the sarong, cut a piece of fabric 59" × 36" (148 × 90 cm). For the patchwork border, cut strips across the width of the fabrics (in other words, so that they are 36" [90 cm]) long). Cut two strips of blue fabric 3" (7.5 cm) wide and two strips each of yellow and green 2" (5 cm) wide.

1 Join fabric strips along their lengths with a ⅝" (1.5 cm) seam, having the blue strips on the outer edges. Press the seams flat.

2 Cut the patchwork across into 2" (5 cm) wide pieces, using a cutting mat, rotary cutter and steel ruler (see page 73). Trim the edge as necessary.

3 Pin the pieces so that the yellow and green patches alternate to create a checkered pattern.

4 Sew the pinned pieces together with ⅝" (1.5 cm) seams. Join enough pieces to make a patchwork strip measuring 36" (90 cm) in length.

5 Press the seams flat.

6 Place the patchwork at one short edge of the main fabric, right sides together, with raw edges matching. Pin.

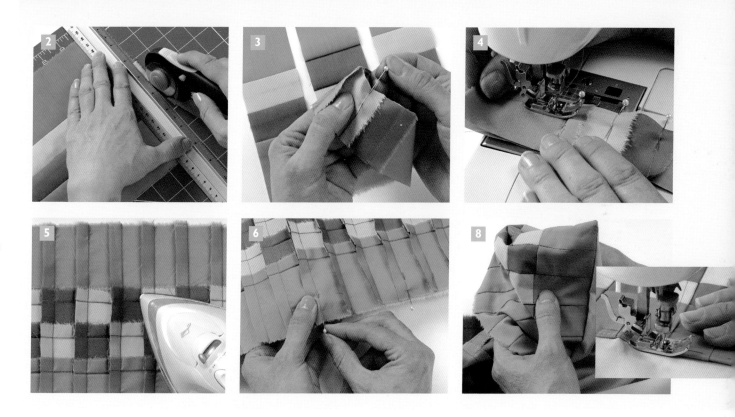

7 Stitch along the top (short) edge, and down the side, ⅝" (1.5 cm) from the raw edges. Leave the bottom edge and the other long edge open.

8 Clip corners and turn right sides out. Press. Turn under ⅝" (1.5 cm) on the raw edge of the patchwork, pin, baste and topstitch.

9 Fold under a double hem at the top

edge. The hem will be on the right side of the fabric, forming a waistband. Pin, baste, and topstitch. Fold under a double hem on the lower edge, with the hem on the wrong side of the fabric; pin, baste, and topstitch.

TIP
With fine cotton fabrics it can be easier and as accurate to tear the fabric across its width than to cut it. Measure the width of the strips along the selvage on the laid out fabric, make a small cut, then tear. This will produce a slightly frayed edge but it does not matter. Always test before tearing.

| CRAZY PATCHWORK
PENNANTS

Crazy patchwork originated as an economical way to patch worn quilts or clothing. The patches are applied in a free-style overlapping design to a foundation fabric. Traditionally, the edges were concealed with embroidery stitches but the patches on these fabulous pennants are edged with zig-zag stitch. Hang them across a room or outdoors to create a festive feel.

You will need

• ¾ yard (70 cm) lightweight cotton fabric, 36" (90 cm) wide, for the foundation fabric

• 8" (20 cm) lengths of six plain and patterned cotton fabrics, each 36" (90 cm) wide

• 3⅓ yards (3.2 m) bias binding, 2" (5 cm) wide

MAKING UP

From the lightweight cotton fabric, cut a 12"(30 cm) wide strip for the backing. Set the remaining fabric aside. From the six assorted fabrics, cut patches in various straight edged shapes.

1 Working across the piece, arrange the patches on the backing fabric, overlapping the edges by ¼" to ⅜" (6 to 8 mm). Pin and baste in place.

2 Stitch the patches to the backing ⅛" (3 mm) inside the raw edges.

3 Set the sewing machine to a close zig-zag stitch about ¼" (5 mm) wide. Stitch over the straight stitches on the patches using contrasting machine embroidery thread. When you reach a corner, lift the presser foot with the needle in the fabric at the outside edge of the zig-zagging. Pivot the fabric so that the work is now facing the new direction and continue. Pull all the thread ends to the wrong side.

4 Pin the patchworked fabric to the remaining backing fabric with right sides facing. Trim the fabrics to a 10½" (26 cm) wide strip. Refer to the cutting diagram to cut eight pennants. Stitch the patchworked fabric pennants together along the slanted edges(leaving the top edge unstitched). Clip the corners, turn right side out and press.

5 Baste the raw top edges of pennants together. Starting 18" (45 cm) from one end of the bias binding, pin the pennants to the wrong side of the binding 4" (10 cm) apart, matching the raw edges to the fold.

6 Fold over the bias binding and baste the long edges together, enclosing the top of the pennants. Stitch close to the long edges with a straight stitch.

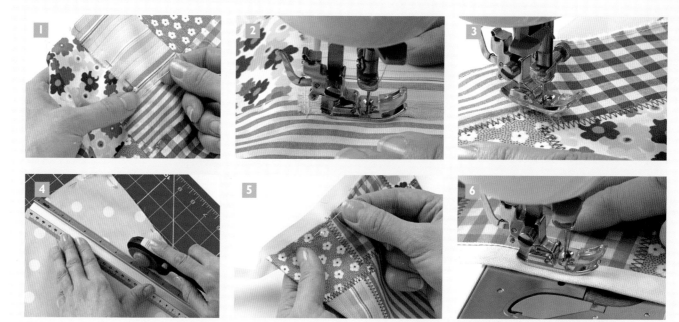

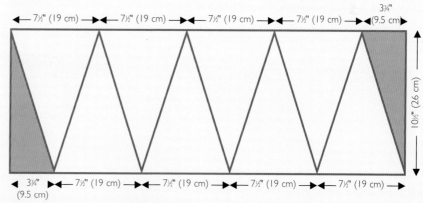

TEMPLATE

Top edge measurements: ← 7½" (19 cm) → ← 7½" (19 cm) → ← 7½" (19 cm) → ← 7½" (19 cm) → ← 3¾" (9.5 cm) →

10½" (26 cm)

Bottom edge measurements: ← 3¾" (9.5 cm) → ← 7½" (19 cm) → ← 7½" (19 cm) → ← 7½" (19 cm) → ← 7½" (19 cm) →

Hand appliqué

By stitching one fabric on top of another, you can create marvellous effects, particularly when combined with quilting. The stitches used to secure the fabric can be invisible or used as part of the decorative effect.

Many different fabrics, stitches, and trims can be used with appliqué though its a good idea to begin by creating a simple design, consisting of a relatively small number of large- or medium-sized pieces constructed mainly of straight lines or gradual curves. You can work out your design, enlarging or reducing it as necessary, and then transfer it to paper from which you can cut out templates. These won't have any seam allowances so mark the exact outline of each piece on your fabric. You can baste lines on your base fabric to help you place the appliqué pieces.

PREPARING THE BASE FABRIC

Cut the fabric 1" (2.5 cm) larger all around than the desired size. Fold in half horizontally, vertically, and then diagonally, and press the folds. Open the fabric and baste along each fold with contrasting thread. Press flat.

MAKING THE APPLIQUÉ

1 Trace the design and label each piece by letter. Make a template for each appliqué. Label each template with the correct letter. Mark the outline of appliqués on the right side of your fabric and cut out, adding a ¼" (5 cm) seam allowance.

2 Use the tip of a sharp pair of scissors to clip into the curved edges perpendicular to the marked outline; do not clip beyond the outline. Make extra clips along deep curves for ease in turning.

3 Using your tracing, pencil the outlines of pieces on to the right side of the base fabric, about ¼" (5 mm) within the outline, to avoid marks showing around the edges.

4 Following the placement lines, arrange your appliqués on the base. Position the background pieces first, then overlap the foreground pieces. Pin or baste the pieces to the base.

5 Turn the raw edges of the appliqués ¼" (5 mm) to the wrong side, using the tip of your needle as a tool for turning.

6 Using matching thread and making tiny invisible slip stitches, sew the appliqués to the base fabric, starting with the background pieces and finishng with the topmost appliqués.

7 Turn the completed design to the wrong side and very carefully cut away the base fabric within all the larger appliqué pieces, leaving a ¼" (5 mm) seam allowance. This eliminates any puckers, and makes quilting easier. Remove the pins and basting threads and press the appliqués lightly on a thick towel.

A sewing machine makes short work of stitching down motifs — and creating details that are too small to make in fabric, such as the veining on leaves or the spots and antennae of ladybugs.

Before starting to sew, make sure to attach a new needle and a zig-zag foot. When adding pieces, use 100 percent cotton thread that matches the color of the appliqué. Technically, you do not need to add an allowance when cutting out your pieces because the seam allowances are not turned under. However, it is not easy to keep the pieces from puckering when stitching very close to the edges. Therefore, the steps shown here show a seam allowance, which is trimmed away after stitching.

Test your stitching on a scrap of fabric. Use a standard width of ⅛" (3 mm) for medium-weight fabrics. Fine fabrics will require a narrower stitch width, and heavy fabrics a wider one. The tension should be even and should not pucker the fabric. If the bobbin thread shows through to the right side, loosen the top tension of the sewing machine.

STITCH EFFECTS

Use machine embroidery stitches, such as satin and zig-zag, to create a variety of embellishments. A highly contrasting thread also will create special effects in machine appliqué, with black or dark gray creating a stained glass appearance.

MAKING THE APPLIQUÉ

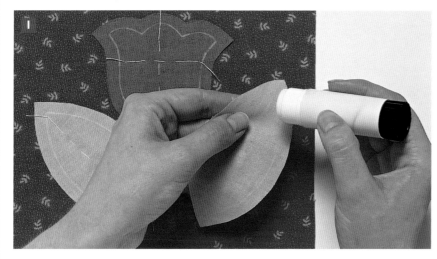

1 Cut out the appliqué and prepare the base as directed on page 78. Follow steps 1, 2, and 4 for Hand appliqué (see page 79). Arrange the pieces in their correct position on the base fabric and attach, using a fabric glue and basting stitches.

2 Machine stitch along the marked outline of each appliqué, using matching thread to make short, straight stitches.

3 Using sharp embroidery scissors, carefully trim away the excess seam allowance beyond the stitching line, cutting as close to your machine stitches as possible.

4 Zig-zag stitch over the line of stitches, covering the raw edges of the fabric. Gently guide the fabric around any curves so the machine sews smoothly. Work slowly so that you have complete control over your stitching.

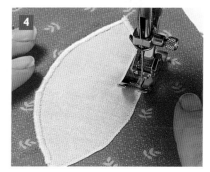

VALLEYS

A sharp dip in an appliqué is called a valley. Clip into the seam allowance to the marked outline. Fold the edges to the wrong side. The seam allowances will separate, leaving virtually no fabric at the valley. Appliqué as normal; when you reach the dip, work a few extra stitches.

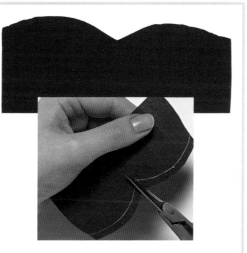

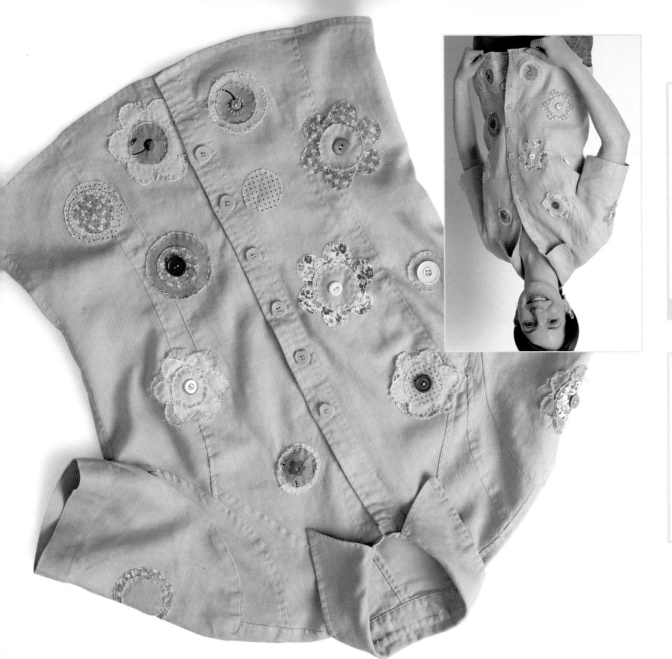

A great way to give new life to a favorite top that's become a bit worn or to decorate a plain shirt is to add an array of fabric motifs, slightly frayed and "distressed" and held in place with decorative stitches and buttons.

You will need

- Plain linen shirt
- Remnants of linen and cotton fabrics, plain and printed
- Lingerie wash bag
- Embroidery floss and sewing thread
- Buttons

MAKING THE SHIRT

1 Make cardboard templates and draw around them on to various fabrics, using a water-soluble marker pen.

2 Cut out each shape. It is a good idea to cut more shapes than you think you will need, to allow a degree of flexibility when arranging them on the shirt, and to allow for any becoming too frayed after following step 3.

3 Place the cut shapes in a lingerie bag and wash in a washing machine to produce the frayed edges. Press with a hot iron to dry.

4 Place the pieces on the shirt, layering, arranging, and rearranging them until you are happy with the design.

5 Pin the motifs in place. Stitch to secure, making sure you sew through all thicknesses of fabric, using a neat running stitch around the edges.

6 Using two strands of contrasting embroidery floss, sew around the edges of some of the shapes using blanket stitch. You may prefer to use a hoop for this. Stitch buttons in the centers of some of the motifs.

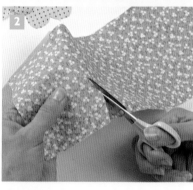

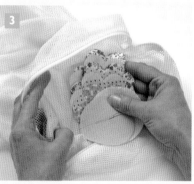

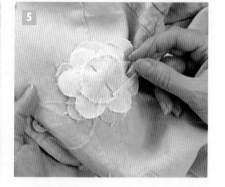

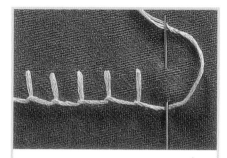

BLANKET STITCH

This is used both for decorative purposes and to reinforce the edges of shapes in danger of raveling.

Work from left to right, bring the thread out near the edge at the position for the looped edging. Insert the needle above and a little to the left of this point, and make a straight onward stitch, with the thread under the tip of the needle. Pull up the stitch to form the loop, then repeat.

TEMPLATE

| # QUILTED BELT

Create a simple silk belt with ribbon ties then dress it up with appliqués cut from patterned fabric. Dot a few beads on top of the "flowers" for extra sparkle.

You will need

- 1 yard (90 cm) silk dupion, 36" (90 cm) wide

- ⅓ yard (30 cm) curtain interlining, 60" (150 cm) wide

- Lightweight cotton fabric with printed large and small motifs

- Bonding web

- Small beads

MAKING THE BELT

1 Enlarge the template below to suit and cut two silk pieces and one interlining piece. Cut six 15" × 1" (38 × 2.5 cm) bias strips of silk for the ties.

2 Pin and baste the interlining centrally to the wrong side of one silk belt. Use a quilting foot on the sewing machine to stitch four lines of quilting ⅝" (1.5 cm) apart along the length of the belt, starting and finishing ⅝" (1.5 cm) from the short edges.

3 Fold the ties lengthwise in half with right sides facing Stitch the long edges, using a ¼" (5 mm) seam allowance. Turn right side out with a bodkin. Turn in one end of each tie and slipstitch the ends together.

4 Pin the raw end of one tie centrally to the ends of the quilted belt. Pin a tie above and below the center tie ¼" (5 mm) apart. Baste in place.

5 With right sides facing, pin and stitch the belts together using a ⅝" (1.5 cm) seam allowance, leaving an opening in the lower edge. Clip the seam allowance across the corners. Trim the interlining in the seam allowance close to the seam. Trim and clip the seam allowances. Turn the belt right side out. Slipstitch the

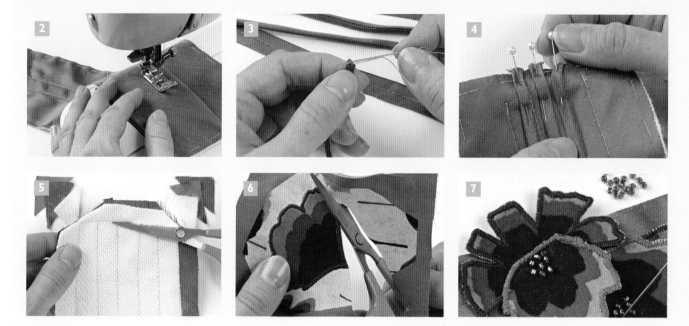

opening closed, Using a warm iron with a cloth on top, press the belt.

6 Roughly cut out nine large motifs and nine small motifs from the printed fabric. Apply the motifs to scraps of the silk dupion with bonding web. Zig-zag along the edges of the motifs with coordinating sewing thread.

7 Arrange the small motifs on the large ones and place in groups of three on the belt. Sew in place with small stitches over the zig-zagging. Sew clusters of eight beads to some of the smaller motifs.

TEMPLATE

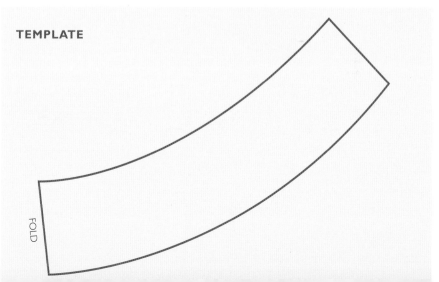

FOLD

A scattering of petals made of a fine closely woven woolen fabric with centers of decorative flower-shaped pearlized buttons can be added to the ends of a hand-made scarf to create a one-of-a-kind accessory. Great to wear or to give as a gift.

You will need

- ⅓ yard (30 cm) rust-colored fine wool or tweed fabric, 60" (150 cm) wide

- ¼ yard (23 cm) pale rust-colored fine wool or tweed, 60" (150 cm) wide

- Matching stranded cotton embroidery floss

- 10 ⅝" (1.5 cm) mother-of-pearl buttons

MAKING UP

Cut out an 8 ⅝" (22 cm) wide strip of the darker colored fabric for the scarf. Cut out four large flowers from both fabrics and six small flowers from the paler fabric.

1 Make the fringe: fray the short edges of the scarf for 3½" (8 cm). Pull away two threads from the long side edges of the scarf. To neaten the side edges, set the sewing machine to a small zig-zag stitch and stitch the side edges, starting and finishing at the fringed ends.

2 Mark the fringed ends with dressmaking pins at ⅜"(8 mm) intervals. Knot each ⅜" (8 mm) section of the fringe close to the scarf.

3 Thread an embroidery needle with three strands of floss. Knot the thread end. Work buttonhole stitch on the ends of the petals by bringing the thread to the right side ⅛" (3 mm) inside one petal edge. Insert the needle back into the fabric ⅛" (3 mm) in from the fabric edge. Loop the thread under the needle point.

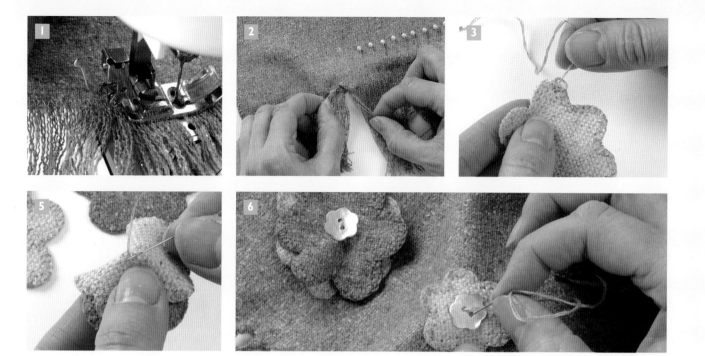

4 Pull the needle and thread and insert the needle back into the fabric ⅛" (3 mm) to the right of where it emerged. Continue forming looped stitches around the edge of the petals, taking care not to pull the thread too tight.

5 Place each darker colored flower on a paler one; alternate the petals. Fold the flowers into quarters; secure with a few stitches at the center, which will pucker the flowers. Open out the petals.

6 Pin two large and three small flowers on each end of the scarf. Sew a button to the center of each appliqué flower with embroidery floss.

TEMPLATE

KEEPSAKE PICTURE

A landmark birthday deserves a special gift such as an appliquéd picture. Choose motifs that will appeal to the recipient and personalize the design with her birth date and initials. You can frame it, but make sure to trim the picture to fit a backing board and glue the picture edges smoothly to the board.

You will need

- ⅓ yard (30 cm) lightweight blue fabric, 36" (90 cm) wide

- ¼ yard (23 cm) lightweight white fabric, 36" (90 cm) wide

- Scraps of four lightweight fabrics

- Bonding web

- 5" (12 cm) silver ribbon, ⅜" (8 mm) wide

- Sequins: 6" (15 cm) strings pink and green, two silver, three yellow flower shaped

- Small blue beads

- Matching sewing thread

- Stranded cotton embroidery floss in silver, pink, and yellow

- Erasable marker

TEMPLATES

| # MAKING THE PICTURE

For the background, cut out a 13" × 9" (33 × 23 cm) rectangle of blue fabric. For the skirt, cut out a 3½" × 2" (9.5 × 5 cm) rectangle from plain fabric, cutting it with the selvage to prevent fraying.

On tracing paper, draw the initials 1½" (4 cm) high by 1¼" (3 cm) wide, and the pair of shoes, drawing the straps separately. Because you are using a motif that is not symmetrical, you need to draw a mirror image of it to apply it with bonding web. Now turn the tracings over and redraw with a black pen.

Trace the upturned initials and shoes on the paper backing side of the bonding web. Also draw three 4½" × 3" (11 × 7.5 cm) rectangles and the bodice, label, and handbag. Roughly cut out the shapes. Iron the rectangles onto the white fabric. Iron all the other pieces onto the wrong sides of the fabric scraps. Cut out the shapes.

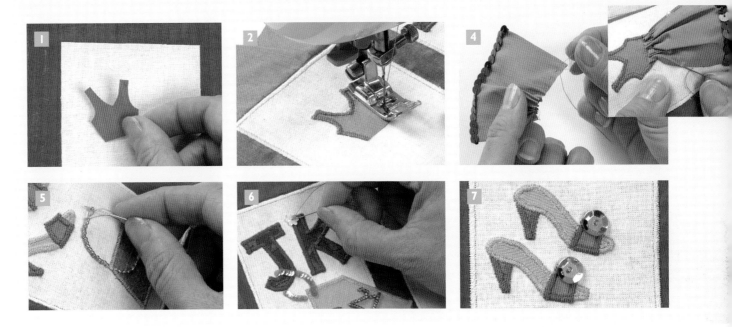

1 Peel the backing papers off the appliqué pieces. Position the white rectangles across the center of the blue fabric ¾" (2 cm) apart. Iron the rectangles to fuse them in place. Set aside the shoe straps. Iron the other pieces in place. Place the straps on the shoes and iron them in position.

2 Set your machine to a close zig-zag stitch. Zig-zag around the rectangles and motifs with matching sewing thread; there is no need to zig-zag the lower edge of the bodice.

3 Press under ¼" (5 mm) on the short edges of the skirt. Sew a string of sequins along the lower raw edge. Gather the upper raw edge of the skirt. Pull up the gathers to ¾" (2 cm).

4 Pin the gathers to the bodice's lower edge. Pin the skirt's pressed edges to the blue fabric, flaring the skirt out from the bodice. Hand sew the skirt in place with

small stitches along the pressed edges and gathers. With an erasable marker, draw the label, label string, coat hanger, handbag handle, and, on the label, the recipients's birth date and age.

5 Using three stands of embroidery floss, backstitch the hanger, birth date, and the handbag flap; use French knots for the dots. To sew small beads along the handbag handle and "21," thread on three beads and lay them along the line. Make a backstitch after the third bead

then insert the needle through it and continue along the line.

6 Sew a row of green sequins for the label string as if it is looped around one initial. Apply a flower-shaped sequin to one initial, the handbag flap, and the dress by bringing up the needle, adding the sequin and bead, and bringing the needle back through the sequin.

7 Repeat as above to sew a silver sequin to each shoe strap. Tie the ribbon into a bow and stitch to the dress, trimming the tails diagonally.

Fine fabrics can be decorated with solid, lace, or net motifs. These are applied to the surface of ground fabric and outlined with hand embroidery to secure them. The ground fabric is then cut away from beneath them, in order to create light behind the motifs and a more interesting effect. As well as commercially available motifs from notions departments, vintage slips are another good source.

EMBROIDERED DECORATION

To augment a motif, stitching can be used to suggest a theme. Here, some French knots and satin stitch leaves have been added to suggest a flower.

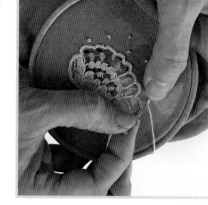

WORKING APPLIQUÉS

LACE APPLIQUÉ

1 Firmly stretch your ground fabric in a hoop and then pin and baste the lace motif on top.

2 Work around the edges of the motif with buttonhole or satin stitch to cover the edges.

3 When the motif is completely outlined, remove the fabric from the frame and cut away the ground fabric from beneath, using blunt ended scissors. If you like, you can further embellish the edges with small dots or sprays of satin stitches.

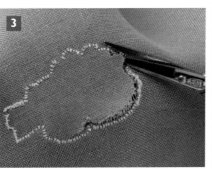

SOLID MOTIF ON NET GROUND

1 Mark the design on your ground fabric and then baste this on top of the net. Stitch over the outlines through both layers, using a closely worked blanket stitch (see page 83).

2 When you have finished stitching, remove the basting threads and cut away the surplus material outside the motif close to the design lines, using blunt-ended scissors.

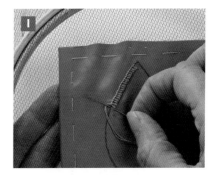

NET MOTIF ON A SOLID GROUND

Mark the design on the ground fabric and then baste the net on top of it. Stitch over the outlines through both layers of fabric using a closely worked blanket stitch (see page 83) and then remove the basting threads. Using blunt-ended scissors, cut away the ground from inside the motif and the excess net around it.

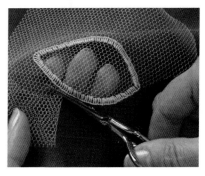

| # TOP WITH LACE MOTIF

Add decorative interest and a touch of luxury to a simple top by applying a lace insert. A butterfly is a delightful motif to use, and once formed, can be highlighted with a scattering of twinkling sequins. Here, the fabric behind the motif is cut away but it can be left intact if you prefer.

You will need

- 6" (15 cm) square lace fabric

- Erasable marker

- 2½" (6 cm) ribbon ⅛" (3 mm) wide

- Sharp, pointed embroidery scissors

- Blunt-ended scissors

- Sequins, optional

| MAKING UP

1 Draw the butterfly on the top with an erasable marker. Pin and baste the lace smoothly to the fabric. If the lace is too dense to see through, the butterfly can be drawn on the lace instead of the camisole. Stitch along the outline and center of the butterfly using short, straight stitches. Remove the basting.

2 Set the sewing machine to a close zig-zag stitch about ⅛" (3 mm) wide. Stitch over the straight stitches of the outline, guiding the fabric around the curves. When you reach a corner, lift the presser foot with the needle in the fabric at the inside edge of the zig-zagging. Pivot the top so the work is now facing the new direction and continue.

3 Pull the thread ends to the back of the work. Thread the ends onto a needle and insert the needle through the zig-zag stitches for about ¾" (2 cm) to secure. Cut off the excess thread.

4 With a sharp pair of embroidery scissors, trim the lace around the motif close to the stitches. Adjust the stitch width on your machine to about 1/16" (1.5 mm) wide. Zig-zag stitch along the antenna. When complete, work the thread ends through the zig-zag stitches on the wrong side as before.

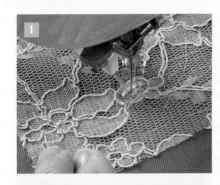

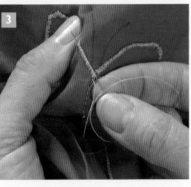

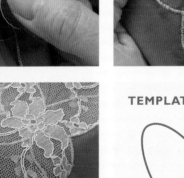

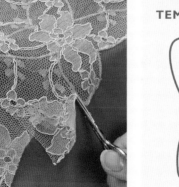

TEMPLATE

5 At each end of the ribbon, press under ⅜" (8 mm). Baste the ribbon along the center of the butterfly to create the body. Adjust the stitch width to 1/20" (1 mm) wide. Zig-zag stitch along the center of the ribbon. Work the thread ends through the zig-zag stitches on the wrong side as before.

6 Carefully cut away the fabric from beneath the lace butterfly with a pair of blunt-ended scissors.

FINISHING TOUCH
If you like, sew some sequins to the motif and scatter the rest close by on the top itself.

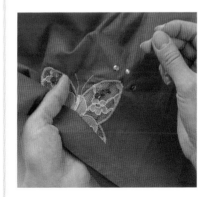

Index

Acknowledgments

Projects created by:

Cheryl Owen

Gwen Diamond

Susie Johns

Template maker:

Amanda Williams

For Carroll & Brown Limited:

Editorial	Amy Carroll
Design	Chrissie Lloyd
	Denise Brown
	Emily Cook
Production	Louise Dixon